Mediumship Romance

THE
REINCARNATION
OF A
QUEEN

Dictated by the Spirit

**John Wilmont
Earl of Rochester**

Psychography of
ARANDI GOMES TEXEIRA

English translation:
Maricarmen Salas Alarcon.
Lima, Peru, May 2023

Original title in Portuguese:

"A reencarnação de uma rainha"

© 2014 Arandi Gomes Teixeira

Translated from the 1st electronic edition, January 2020

World Spiritist Institute

Houston, Texas, USA

E–mail: contact@worldspiritistinstitute.org

INDEX

PROLOGUE……………………………………………..	13
1.- FATHER AND SON………………………………..	16
2.- PANDERVA…………………………………………..	40
3.- THE COURT AND THE NOBLEMAN………………	65
4.- THE PROVINCIAL COURT……………………....	73
5.- THEOBALD………………………………………...	75
6.- PROVOCATIONS………………………………….	79
7.- DREAM AND REALITY…………………………..	81
8.- PACT………………………………………………...	82
9.- MATTHEW AND CYRENE………………………..	85
10.- THE MUSE………………………………………..	90
11.- PROVIDENTIAL ZEAL…………………………..	97
12.- OBSESSION……………………………………..	109
13.- THE INTERVIEW…………………………………..	116
14.- MR. ANASTACIO…………………………………..	124
15.- THE BELOVED DAUGHTER……………………..	128
16.- COMFORTABLE AND WELL SERVED…………	134
17.- THE AGREEMENT………………………………...	144
18.- METAPHYSICS…………………………………...	152
19.- CONVIVIENCE…………………………………...	157
20.- COUNT FERNANDO……………………………..	159
21.- MOTHER AND DAUGHTER……………………..	163
22.- THE ENGAGEMENT……………………………..	178
23.- THE OCCASION…………………………………..	184

24.– THE POWER OF THE PAST...............................	195
25.– THE LETTER..	201
26.– THE CARDINAL'S DEPARTURE.......................	208
27.– WISDOM...	210
28.– MALICIOUS INTERESTS.................................	218
29.– THE RISKS..	222
30.– STRANGE DIALOGUE.....................................	231
31.– USELESS SEARCH...	241
32.– THE REINITIATION..	246
33.– THE GREAT REVOLT OF THEOBALD...............	259
34.– THE NEMESIS...	278
EPILOGUE...	281

About the Medium

Arandi Gomes Texeira is an incarnated spirit conscious that she must evolve, materially and spiritually, to dignify her own existence.

In 1975, she looked for a Spiritist house to help one of her children. She began to study intensely the works of Allan Kardec, in which she found answers to old questions. After the spiritual treatment of her son, she stayed in the Spiritist house, with the purpose of assuming, intellectually and morally, the principles and postulates of the Spiritist Doctrine.

Her childhood and adolescence were full of phenomena; some of them physical, terrifying and even aggressive. Then she learned to live with both planes of life. Once in the Spiritist Doctrine, she decided to study her mediumship, educate it and exercise it in the Spiritist work.

In the late 1970s, a neighbor almost "forced" her to read a large book with a silver cover. At first, she refused to do so due to lack of time, but at his insistence, she leafed through it. One afternoon, she decided to check it out. The book was "The Revenge of the Jew." She says that right at the beginning of the reading she felt strange, emotional, and began to get angry, inexplicably, with this or that. She asked herself, "Arandi, have you gone crazy?" How could she be so demanding? She didn't know the book, had never heard of it and didn't even know the name of its author. So she checked it out and read, "John Wilmot, Earl of Rochester." The impact was great. What a strange situation!... Arandi says that at that moment an idea came to her: challenge the author... She asked him, in a loud and clear voice: "Come to me! Manifest yourself...! I did not have to invoke him twice. He materialized in the middle of the room, smiling, dressed in the clothes of an English nobleman, showing great joy. So, we were looking at each other. I was crying, a lot, and he was very happy. From then on, we never really parted."

Other phenomena arose and they began to walk together every night during her out-of-body experiences. "We wandered, many times, through different spaces and spheres; we talked a lot and he instructed me on the works I should study. Eventually, he told me that we would write books. So it was and so it has been."

On his connection to Earl J.W. Rochester, she explains: "My connection with this spirit is very old. We have walked side by side for a long time. We know each other quite well and respect each other deeply. Yes, there are many facts and countless revelations of other reincarnations, in the different periods he focuses on in his books."

Regarding Rochester's style and the use of various mediums, Arandi indicates that "in fact, Rochester's style is unmistakable. Highly appreciated, he has a very eclectic audience. As for other mediums, it is up to the reader to analyze, compare the works and draw his or her own conclusions.

The work of psychography is, almost always, exciting. At the end of the work, there are many tears, thanks to the author and there is also the satisfaction of having succeeded to carry out the work despite the obstacles. We never say goodbye. While I make the endless revisions and plans for the desirable edits, he is there, participating in everything, always."

The mediumistic novels allow those interested in Spiritism to know Kardec's work, so much so that those who do not study Spiritism may not understand the Spiritist novels at all. Rochester always bases his works on the codification of Allan Kardec (his friend since the time of ancient Egypt). We can, with justice, consider him one of the precursors of Spiritism, when he narrates stories of the ancient world and explains mediumistic phenomena, demonstrating an admirable knowledge of the spiritual plane.

Arandi does not see any inconvenience in mediumistic novels when they are based on spiritist principles and postulates. When they are not, they may be novels, but they will never be spiritist. Her advantage lies in her objectives: to entertain, to make people dream, to thrill, to surprise, to instruct, to enlighten and to point out directions, educating and transforming. Our beloved author knows, like no one else, how to create, weave plots and develop them, with mastery, in real stories or not; it doesn't matter, because, according to him, life is more fantastic than fiction.

Finally, she says that when she works on the novels of the beloved John Wilmot, Earl of Rochester, she is the first to benefit from the light he gives her and the incomparable opportunity to work and learn.

Excerpted from "Interview with Arandi Gomes Texeira" by Eliana Haddad, April 13th, 2020

Published in Correio.news by Correio Fraterno

URL: https://correio.news/leitura/entrevista-arandi-gomes

About the Spiritual Author

John Wilmot Rochester was born on April 1st or 10th, 1647 (there is no record of the exact date). He was the son of Henry Wilmot and Anne (widow of Sir Francis Henry Lee), Rochester was similar to his father in physique and temperament: dominant and proud. Henry Wilmot received the title of Earl because of his efforts to raise money in Germany to help King Charles I regain the throne after he was forced to leave England.

When his father died, Rochester was 11 years old and inherited the title of Earl, with little inheritance and honors.

Young J.W. Rochester grew up in Ditchley in the midst of benders, theatrical intrigues, artificial friendships with professional poets, lust, brothels in Whetstone Park and the friendship of the king, whom he despised.

For the time, he had a vast culture: he mastered Latin and Greek, knew the classics, French and Italian, was the author of satirical poetry, highly appreciated in his time.

In 1661, at the age of 14, he graduated from Wadham College, Oxford, with a Master of Arts degree. He then left for France and Italy and became an interesting figure: tall, slim, attractive, intelligent, charming, brilliant, subtle, educated and modest, ideal characteristics to conquer the frivolous society of his time.

When he was not yet 20 years old, in January 1667, he married Elizabeth Mallet. Ten months later, drinking began to affect his character. He had four children with Elizabeth and a daughter, in 1677, with the actress Elizabeth Barry.

Living the most different experiences, from fighting against the Dutch navy on the high seas to being involved in crimes of death, Rochester's life followed paths of madness, sexual abuse, alcoholism and charlatanism, in a period in which he served as a "doctor".

When Rochester was 30 years old, he writes to a former adventuring companion that he was nearly blind, lame and unlikely to return to London.

Quickly recovering, Rochester returned to London. Shortly thereafter, in agony, he set out on his last adventure: he called the priest Gilbert Burnet and dictated his memories to him. In his last reflections, Rochester acknowledged having lived a wicked life, which ended slowly and painfully because of the venereal diseases that dominated him.

Earl of Rochester died on July 26th, 1680. In the state of spirit, Rochester received the mission to work for the propagation of Spiritualism, and he did so after 200 years through the medium Vera Kryzhanovskaia. The automatism that characterized her made her hand trace words with dizzying speed and total unconsciousness of ideas. The narratives that were dictated to her denote a wide knowledge of ancestral life and customs and provide in their details such a unique style and historical truth that it is difficult for the reader not to recognize their authenticity. Rochester proves to dictate his historical-literary production, testifying that life unfolds to infinity in its indelible marks of spiritual memory, towards the light and the way of God. It seems impossible for a historian, however erudite, to study, simultaneously and in depth, times and environments as different as the Assyrian, Egyptian,

Greek and Roman civilizations; as well as customs as dissimilar as those of the France of Louis XI to those of the Renaissance.

The theme in Rochester's work begins in Pharaonic Egypt, moves through Greco-Roman antiquity and the Middle Ages, and continues into the 19th century. In his novels, reality navigates in a fantastic current, in which the imaginary surpasses the limits of verisimilitude manifesting natural phenomena that oral tradition has perpetuated as supernatural.

Rochester's referential is full of content about customs, laws, ancestral mysteries and unfathomable facts of history, under a novelistic layer, where social and psychological aspects pass through the sensitive filter of his great imagination. Rochester's classification of genre is hampered by his expansion into several categories: gothic horror with romance, family sagas, adventures and forays into the fantastic.

The number of editions of Rochester's works, spread over countless countries, is so large that it is not possible to have an idea of their magnitude, especially considering that, according to researchers, many of these works are unknown to the general public.

Several lovers of Rochester's novels carried out (and perhaps still do) searches in libraries in various countries, especially in Russia, to find yet-unknown works. This can be seen in the transcribed prefaces of several works. Many of these works are finally available in Spanish thanks to the **World Spiritist Institute.**

Only moral progress can assure people of happiness on the earth by restraining evil passions. It alone can enable harmony, peace and fraternity to reign.

Allan Kardec

The Genesis – chap. 18, item 19

PROLOGUE

Dear readers!

At that time, in which our novel is set, the multiple characters already instinctively and courageously structured the brilliant stage of the Renaissance, which would come to the rescue of arts and culture, thought and science, irremediably with the excesses resulting from all that is new and still misunderstood and subjected to the onslaught of human passions.

Vigilant and loyal to God and to life, committed to Truth, these champions of true progress were fertile ground, in which would be sown the seeds of Good and Love, which would travel in the chariot of triumph to institute a new era on our planet.

In an unequal and implacable fight, they collided with those who fiercely clung to false values or any moral values, suffering, as a consequence, cruel reprisals. An immense theater, sometimes horrific, sometimes sublime, was installed in all spheres of life and the combat became overwhelming and savage.

For a long time, the clergy, possessors of power and of all possible and imaginable prerogatives, have cruelly dominated.

Jealous of their positions of relevance, these pseudo-leaders have assembled a powerful and wide network, like a monstrous snake, which hungry and thirsty attacks those who, by chance, dare to challenge it.

Day by day, life at that time proceeded in the midst of outrages of all kinds.

But lo and behold, a dawn of gradual and broad change was announced, bringing wholesome hope and joy to the hearts that struggled for the establishment of order and true justice.

The ruling power, however, was imposing itself with arrogance, taking what it wanted and doing what it pleased. Disoriented and obstinate in evil, while soaked in the tears and blood of others, they created for themselves unimaginable pains and sufferings, which would extend for countless reincarnation expiations.

It is worth remembering that, considering the evolutionary journey of all of us, immortal spirits towards perfection, when we are repentant and after countless fights, many of us may have reached much higher evolutionary levels in less time than other souls, who already identify with good, but remain in indolence and complacency.

And who among us can know where one has been and what one has done in so much time traveled? After so many centuries – this no longer matters –, we have to assume new times, new ideas and ideals, in line with the will of the Creator.

Wherever we may go and wherever we have lived, we leave footprints and traces of our actions.

In this tiny world, we live our days, now lost in memory, benefiting from the kindness of the Lord's agents, who gave us new opportunities to grow and evolve.

In the learning process, like students returning to school benches, thirsty for love, we followed the paths traced towards the desirable redemption that would unfold over time, but in our own way.

Recalcitrant, we act as we want and not as we should, in unbridled rebellion.

Making use of our well-developed intelligence, and nostalgic for the comforts to which we were accustomed, we were intensely driven to development and creation that would guarantee us the perpetuity of comforts and pleasures, while we struggled to establish our way of being and living, for which, marginalized, many of us were purged from other worlds.

Woe to us! How much time wasted! Only pain would make us stop and reflect.

Yet, when we look back, we see with shame that after so long we are still slow to get it right and eager to exercise our old addictions.

Today, immersed in a historical phase, due to the transition from a world of trials and atonements to a world of regeneration, evil is concentrated in dark and apocalyptic synergies.

Thus, with great difficulty, we painfully reap the result of our former sowing.

More sensitized, today we are surprised by the pain and afflictions that reach almost everyone and we think that we have been wronged. What a mistake! The Creator's justice is perfect, even if we do not have the measures to evaluate it. If we suffer, we should know that pain is often corrected by the right adjustment of ourselves with our conscience, taking into consideration that we are in the great law of cause and effect.

May we not lose; however, the faith and hope that should always guide us, believing that better times will come. Fatal is the progress of creatures and worlds, for nothing in Nature remains stationary. Evil is transient, part of the process of evolution.

When the time is right, progress will come, regardless of any other circumstances, and it will be established forever, officializing the New Age in the name of a higher law, based on love and truth!

John Wilmont, Earl of Rochester

1.– FATHER AND SON

Leaning over his desk, Wladimir Vladosk was extremely resentful:

– "What kind of news was that and why had it not reached his ears before? Was the feudal lord looking for him? What did he want? Was he someone unaccounted for and adrift?

Rumors of a new sedition[1] run through the streets of Florence, and in between, ruin seems to threaten everyone.

A dark and heavy cloud looms in the air.

Will his home be safe from this possible threat? How could he know?"

He flails like a fish out of water and almost loses his breath. Oppressed, he clutches his chest with both hands. He leans back against the back of the old hardwood chair, closes his eyes, and internalizes his thoughts.

It seems like yesterday... He arrived full of dreams but without resources. However, confident and willing to occupy a prominent place in that majestic city, which had inhabited his thoughts several years ago, and with the intention of establishing the proper means to achieve the level of a gentleman, he elaborated his life routine.

But he did not just want to get rich. His aspirations went far beyond that. His morale and intellect, stimulated as always, would continue to develop like cedar.

---

[1] Crime against the State security.

From that moment on, he remembers the unbearable pain in his back, in his still vigorous arms, in his feet that burned on contact with the ground, in the calluses on his hands, on the crown of his head, from carrying such heavy loads. His body ached and needed a rest that was not always possible.

Under the rigors of time, he faced everything to reach his desired level, as well as obtaining the means for a dignified survival. From one village to another and another, he worked doing the most diverse jobs and negotiating goods he transported.

Incomparable learning, constant work, sweat for daily bread!

And just like a background, the most important goals. Numerous steps to accomplish, intense dreams and great intellectual pretensions. At the expense of much sweat, pain, tears, humiliations, shortcomings, facing multiple dangers, accumulating a great amount of money, he was finally able to bargain, negotiate, compete ...

Despite his fatigue, he continued educating himself with so much determination and anxiety, tenaciously immersing himself in the various science of all times, expanding the knowledge he had already acquired since childhood.

He masters a great deal of knowledge. He is able to speak on the most diverse subjects related to almost all sciences.

His contemporaries respect his undeniable competence, his enviable professional prestige and, why not say it, his fortune too.

Throughout all stages of his life, he met people of all kinds and learned to select them, thus preserving the best ones and carefully excluding those who followed tortuous paths. For them he felt great mercy. They are sons of the Almighty in an atmosphere of apprenticeship, still lost in themselves.

To be fair, he should never forget that these people too, because of different circumstances, were of help at decisive moments. Nobody is all good or bad.

He tried not to make enemies, but he had them. Some opposed him for no reason. They would not try to understand, for in their minds there was only interest in the literal meaning of physical existence.

Thus absorbed, Wladimir, who had just written another of his metaphysical theses, did not even notice the approach of his son Norbert, who reverently, was looking at him.

His son admires him for his stoicism in the face of so many challenges and disaffections.

As an upright and determined man, Wladimir always follows the principles of goodness and love, at any time or place. Thanks to God's mercy, he and his father have survived many dangers.

His mother was gone too soon! Poor woman... Valuable mother and admirable wife...

This memory still causes him almost physical pain and his eyes fill with tears. In spite of the time that has passed, he still remembers the sad farewell.

Along with his father, he faces the difficulties of every day, but his soul suffers and struggles with great insecurity. They are so connected that, even from a distance, they seem to communicate mysteriously.

Norbert walks away slowly and silently, leaving him to his thoughts.

He asks the Almighty for him. Only the Creator can grant you all that you need and deserve. Smiling slightly, he imagines how much God must love his father.

Absorbed in himself, he continues walking down the halls:

– "How many times have we survived so far? Some in an extraordinary way: due to the political, moral or financial strength of a friend who, appearing providentially, had pulled us out of the problems that the world knows how to prepare so well to steal from us the precious opportunity to live and grow..."

In the same mood, he walks for some time through a peristyle. In the center, there was a lush garden.

He decides to enjoy the beauty of the flowers, the freshness and lightness of the greenery, the smell of damp soil and the benefits of the balsamic air. He walks down some stone steps and approaches a comfortable bench. He sits down and his deep blue velvet garments are spread out on the seat. His beret of the same fabric and color falls elegantly over his broad, noble forehead.

His big hands with thin, white, slender fingers – despite his usual willingness to do any job – nervously grip the edges of the beautiful, rich bench surface.

With a restless soul, he longs to protect his father and also to feel safer. At every step, dangers and urgency of constant vigilance.

✷ ✷ ✷

Persistent persecution haunts community life. Rude and salaried individuals commit criminal acts in the service of certain institutions as guilty as themselves. To become their victim, it is enough to possess something that interests them (which does not need to be valuable, since addiction unfortunately becomes a compulsion) or to interfere in the interests of someone powerful and accustomed to remain at the top of society.

Often protected by distinguished individuals, these executioners act freely; however, when they fall into disgrace, they begin to annoy those they had just served. Then, the executers make sure these people begin to suffer the same evils they imposed on others.

✷ ✷ ✷

They have already escaped from several ambushes. On some occasions they were wounded; other times, they had to react in order to survive.

There is a patent fatigue in his very young soul that turns into a long and deep sigh.

With the same intention to recover, his father goes over there and, surprising him, sits down next to him, bringing him out of his ecstasy.

– Why are you so thoughtful?

Smiling, Norbert answered warmly:

– It seems to me that today we are both immersed in riddles that are difficult to solve.

– I assume that you observed me a moment ago? Why didn't you talk to me?

– I respected your internalization. I was at the door, quiet, and then I came here.

– Tell me, if you can, what is the reason of your sullen face?

– Some matters bother me a lot... What about you, father?

– I am anxious, and rightly so! My soul is quite restless, son...

– Do you foresee greater dangers than we're used to? I know the rumors and I am also feeling uneasy!

– You could not ignore them, of course, because like me you move daily in your public functions. In these last days, we are more watched than before... I foresee storms... It is not that we have something to hide, but we know the wiles of our enemies...

– Rest! Once again we will be able to overcome the challenges, my father!

Wladimir embraces him by the shoulders, while he concludes paternally:

– You are right! God will preserve and hold us to fulfill our dearest aspirations!

Norbert hold the hand placed on his shoulder, in agreement with what he heard, and remains silent.

Wladimir takes a deep breath, enjoying the pleasant scent of flowers and also immerses himself in his thoughts.

Ignoring each other's thoughts, they recall a traumatic and almost fatal event that marked them forever: together they walked through a town square that had beautiful houses at its surroundings, very crowded at that hour.

They walked hurriedly minding their business, when a group of soldiers who were having fun at the expense of passers-by, saw them and exchanged glances...

At that time, Wladimir was not yet forty and Norbert was almost ten.

Careful, they hurried their pace and were already approaching a corner, when one of them, reckless, decided to chase them.

They looked at each other in silence and very worried. They realized they had to be brave and very cautious. That attack, so unexpected, could be fatal to them.

Their hearts beat strong and wildly like runaway racehorses.

Wladimir still remembers, with a deep and never forgotten pain, the look of his son asking for help and protection.

He encouragingly smiled at him, but an icy chill ran down his back. He feared, especially for him, still so small and so helpless... He knew what cruel people were capable of and those soldiers, in addition to their extremely rough appearance, it was clear by their faces that they had drunk alcohol; some more, some less.

He held his son's hand, giving him confidence, while seeking strength within himself. That reality; however, exceeded any hope of help and salvation, but he continued to smile at him, wordlessly asking him to remain calm.

Norbert responded with effort to his father's expectations. They quickened their pace and were almost running, when the one who was pursuing them reached them.

The others ran and, in a few moments, father and son felt rough, greedy hands grabbing them by their clothes, almost lifting them off the ground.

Wladimir turned to the one giving the orders and, in simple and objective words, explained who he was, where he lived and where he was going.

But like a bull blindly attacking his opponent, he saw only what he could benefit from, stealing their belongings and their opportunity to have a good day. In another state, perhaps, he would have acted differently, but the alcohol clouded his reasoning ability.

He shouted at them to take off their rich, elegant and clean clothes, which interested him very much. Vain, he already imagined himself well dressed and very elegant for the accomplishment he was now undertaking:

"If Aristophanes could only guess with whom I have spent my nights! Ah...! And how gorgeous is that beautiful Greek! In my arms, she finds more love and more passion...! I will take her once and for all! He can stay with his Church, which he seems to love more than anything else in life...! "

Self-absorbed, he becomes detached from the reality around him and, meanwhile, practically naked, ashamed and humiliated, father and son have become the butt of jokes and mockery.

Following the "procedures of law", the henchmen[2] gave them more suitable clothing, in accordance with their conditions as convicts.

Huddled in a corner, father and son watched as some of them arrived, holding the infamous and well-known *sambenitos*[3] that revealed their cruel intentions.

A superlative horror seized them both. Were they saying goodbye and for good?!

Norbert looked at his perplexed father, who, in shock, without losing hope, said to him:

– Be brave, my son, it will pass... Think deeply of God and pray for us with your childlike innocence. He will help us, do not doubt it. If I love you so much, imagine how much He loves his children!...

He could say no more, because the soldiers were already putting the greasy and abominable *sambenitos* on them.

Finally satisfied, those potential executioners laughed to see them dressed in coarse dark clothes, with their bare feet, and ropes tied around their waists.

---

[2] A faithful follower of low level.
[3] Hooded clothing that the convicts were forced to wear as a form of punishment and public defamation.

The one who had initiated the persecution, confident that he had them in his hands, felt bored, so he decided to continue drinking while thinking about what to do to get more fun.

He sat down on the floor and poured the drink down his neck.

Time was torturously passing for father and son. Silently, they looked around, hoping for something that might help them.

The "commander" drank and clicked his tongue with pleasure, and the more he drank, the thirstier he became.

Meanwhile, his men organized themselves around him as best they could, setting here and there with so much indiscipline, as they waited for the orders that were sure to come.

After what seemed an interminable time for father and son, Diogenes – that was the leader's name – struggling to get on his feet, took a deep breath and looked around.

With a smirk, he fixed his already somewhat clouded gaze on them and decided it was time to move on with his criminal intentions.

He walked and shook his head, accepting or rejecting thoughts, seeming to "dialogue" with unseen companions.

Finally, after this irrational confabulation, composed of marches and countermarches, he declared:

– We will challenge these two scoundrels to a very difficult test!
Yes, this is a great idea...!

With a derisive laughter, he added:

– If you comply with our requests, we will be generous, if not! you will go, but without clothes...! It will be quite funny to see you running through the streets as you came into the world.

He bursts out laughing at the images he begins to visualize in his sick mind.

His real desire; however, was to prolong his time of entertainment with his soldiers; weak and pusillanimous men, just like him, since father and sons' fate was already sealed.

He addresses the others and announces with great pride:

– Very well! Let us begin!

– Yes! Let this test begin soon!

His subordinates responded in unison.

– Let everyone know that it will be a great challenge! Those unwinnable ones! After all, we do not want them to run away, do we?

– No! We do not...!

– Well, here's the thing: the two of you must get to the other side of the square in the time we set...! If you do, you will be free! King's word!

Seeing their expressions, Diogenes bursts into uncontrollable laughter.

Meanwhile, the others look at each other in understanding. After all, anyone could easily gain the way between one side of the street and the other...!

Reckless, one of them dares to say:

– But, sir, this is too easy!

Turning to him in anger, which makes the others step back, Diogenes says:

– Wait till I complete my thought, stupid! Do you want to start dancing too? Hum... It would be much more fun! The three of you sweating side by side to win the race! In the end, you would get the laurels or the punishment too! Do you want to try it?

– No, my lord, have mercy! – Begs the man, kneeling in the middle of the street...

Giving a threatening look to him, Diogenes remains silent as he studies the reactions of his subordinates. He likes the impact he causes when he acts like this. He is delighted to observe their fear and the "respect" they pay him.

He does not respond, just gives the supplicant a look that freezes him. He crawls silently to a corner of the street to huddle there, like a reptile. He knows well how cruel Diogenes can be.

Continuing, the "boss" expands his idea:

– You will be able to cross the street to the other side, but...

He cannot complete his idea because he bursts into new and loud guffaws, in a fit of uncontrollable laughter.

Every time he tries to speak to give them the necessary explanations, laughter takes over.

Finally, he takes take a deep breath and explains:

– To cross the street, you will take a step forward, but at the same time... –. He pauses and observes the effect of his words, between new guffaws, holds his big belly to contain himself and continues:

– You will take a step forward and then two steps backwards...! And so it will be: back and forth, back and forth, back and forth, endlessly! We, of course, will be counting the allotted time and with each attempt to deceive us, they will give you what you deserve...!

The other henchmen, just as bad as he was, burst into raucous laughter.

Increasingly enthusiastic, Diogenes continues to expand his unbridled joy, affirming:

– Whenever you need it, we will give you a "little push", won't we?

– Yes! – They all answered.

– And do not try to deceive us! – Said another one, encouraging the "commander" more and more.

– And do not dare to run away, because we know why you are being penalized for, don't we?

Mischievous and treacherous, Diogenes looks at his henchmen meaningfully, waiting for a satisfactory answer.

Looking at each other fearfully, the group mulls over his statements and in a small uproar, they say:

– Well, well, we certainly know, don't we?

Meanwhile, the one who had been threatened decides to take the opportunity to correct his imprudence of minutes ago and at the same time, mischievously, says:

– Our admirable commander must have already elaborated in his powerful mind the due accusation and fair judgment, mustn't he? What would we all be without his undeniable wisdom and competence!

Caught in his own trap, Diogenes is silent. He scratches his greasy head, breathes noisily, and the minutes that generate enormous expectation in his subordinates affect much more Wladimir and Norbert, who with growing horror fear the next insanities of that evil, drunken and completely uncontrolled man.

Finally, emphatically puffing out his chest, Diogenes decided:

– Yes! That's it! They are two heretics! We are witnesses that they made gestures and strange whispers with demonic evocations!

The soldiers agree with these statements, although they all know that the commander is only creating a false defamation to justify his persistent cruelty that feeds on other people's pain.

Father and son look at each other. Where did he get that idea from?!

– Do not lose heart, my son – whispers Wladimir in Norbert's ear–. Keep on praying. If it is God's will, we will emerge unscathed.

All around them, the noise grew louder and louder:

– Heretics! Witches!

– Oh, you scum! Scum of hell! – reproached some people spitting on the ground –. The more we kill them, the more they reproduce!

Motivated and moved by brutality, some rushed towards the two and began to attack them.

Wladimir covers his son with his body, but without mercy, the small group surround them from all sides.

Hugging tightly, they react as best they can.

Norbert cries. Disconsolate and panicked, he presses himself against his father. Never in his entire life had Wladimir suffered so much. His heart bleeds...

After a few minutes of pleasure watching the sad spectacle, Diogenes orders:

– All right, let's get started! You two there! – He points his finger at father and son –. Take one step forward and then two steps back, without a break, until you reach the other side of the square!

Given the "sentence", he smiles with satisfaction:

– If you slow down or try to deceive us, you will be executed right here!

Ruthless echoes harmonized with his lines:

– And do not try to deceive us!

Those who came attracted by the "spectacle" were soon informed of their sin and of the test to which they were being subjected.

Paradoxically, crying out to heaven and blaspheming, they demand the condemnation and execution of the two.

With no way out, silent and terrified, father and son begin to carry out the orders received. In agile steps, they try to reach the goal that was proposed to them without success, because it is impossible to reach the other side of the square in the allotted time.

Wladimir knew that he and his son were only victims of a cruel game.

Among the spectators, only few observed with mercy their evident fragility and the group's arbitrariness. The majority, insensitive, are infected with the same feelings. Thus, the number of people who accuse and condemn, while hiding their own moral miseries, increases.

What are they waiting for? Strong emotions that take them out of the dark life in which they live immersed. They take revenge on others for their own wrongs, unable to forget, however, they are subject to the same injustices.

✲✲✲

We are still, dear readers, close to the feelings and emotions that dominated the Roman circuses witnessing the sacrifices of the Christians.

It is sad to remember the multitude – and how many of us among them? –, who demanded more and more amusement in the same molds and characteristics, although their souls bled with pain for their own miseries...

***

After a while, exhausted, scratched and with pain all over their bodies from the blows they had received, Wladimir and Norbert looked at each other deeply depressed, almost saying goodbye...

Meanwhile, Diogenes had decided to drink more. From that moment on, everything would happen naturally and his subordinates would know how to carry out whatever was pending. That was their way to proceed.

In the end, very drunk, he ended up sleeping: body slumped, mouth open, drool falling on the stones of the street.

Free to act, the soldiers decided to make better use of all that fun situation.

When Diogenes awoke from his drunkenness, they would have convenient and convincing explanations about the conclusion of the case.

Although Wladimir carefully analyzed the situation, he could no longer evaluate how to proceed and how this dangerous situation would end.

He looked up once more at the sky, gazing at the daylight and the free white clouds... With his heart weeping, he concluded that Norbert would not endure much longer.

A heavy sweat ran down the inside of those rough, uncomfortable garments.

With unbearable sadness, he stares at his son, not knowing what to do, noticing his visible weakness.

His beautiful face, reddened and swollen from the slaps he had received, was soaked with tears and stained with everything that was mercilessly thrown at them.

His gaze, usually full of brightness, vanished, revealing great desperation and lack of physical strength.

His little head, always held high and dignified, bent to the ground, limply.

In an attempt to help him, Wladimir was pushed violently and ordered to continue at the same pace.

The laughter of the henchmen burst out and the jokes revealed their eagerness for the consummation of what they were wildly foreshadowing.

Finally, as heavy tears bathe his bruised and dirty face, Wladimir silently cries out to the sky.

And lo and behold, something unexpected happens:

From one of the corners appears an imposing army corps headed by someone who was undoubtedly above everything that happened there or anywhere else in that flourishing city.

The leader, well-dressed as a peacock and strong as an oak, tried to move forward. By this time, he had other interests and was in a hurry. However, he quickly observed those two, dressed in the clothes of the condemned, marching back and forth, completely exhausted.

Concluding that the order must be maintained at any cost, he decided to leave, thinking:

"They must be two poor devils who opposed public authority or were caught committing a serious offense!" Bored with the spectacle, he ordered the retreat.

However, as he approached, one of his subordinates stopped and pointed to something, calling his attention:

– Look, Mr. Aristophanes! There...! Isn't Diogenes that drunkard asleep who is lying like a slaughtered pig on the sidewalk? He must be celebrating with his equals, the demonds!

Pausing his walk, Aristophanes stares at the inert, fallen body and recognizes it:

– Ah, that rogue! We have scores to settle, let's do it! – He hisses, as he angrily stares at his vulnerable and completely helpless enemy. Glaring at him, he spits sideways. He heads towards the henchmen and the small crowd moves away, as he is a well-known and feared figure.

Aristophanes addresses the soldiers who are in charge of the situation and loudly demands urgent explanations.

One of them, pale and trembling, explains:

– Very dear and honored sir! In fulfillment of our duty, we are punishing these two heretics, as required by law!

– And who is your superior, soldier?

Timidly, he points to Diogenes who is lying on the ground.

– Go back to the military unit you belong to. I will handle this situation!

The men, bowing exaggeratedly, leave everything behind and organize a retreat. In this way they leave almost running and stumbling to finally disappear in the adjacent streets, one after the other.

Aristophanes turns to Diogenes and intentionally brings his horse closer. The horses' hooves pound on the cobblestones.

He comes very close to Diogenes, almost stepping on him. A strange smile appears on his lips...

The audience, in suspense, waits. Some with the expectation of seeing Diogenes fighting and being defeated. Aristophanes' will is no different either. However, he controls himself and restrains his own impulses. He needs him alive to settle an old and very particular dispute.

He pulls his sword out of the scabbard, bends down and strikes him violently.

Diogenes is startled and tries to get up, but is unable to. His legs do not obey him. He collapses again as he struggles to identify where the blow came from, but his reddened eyes roll in their sockets, aimlessly. In a few moments, he falls asleep again, lying there on the ground.

Aristophanes shouts angrily:

– Put him on the horse's back and carry him away! When he wakes up, let me know!

Then, pointing to the crowd, he orders:

– Get them out of here! Send them away! Bunch of good-for-nothings! Vultures! Always looking for carrion! Get out! Out! Out!

Then he casually approaches the "condemned" and analyzes them in silence. Then, very surprised, he exclaims:

– Well, well! the wise and powerful Wladimir Vladosk and his son Norbert!

Wladimir does not speak. He has already recognized him, but he doubts what consequences might follow. Perhaps they have escaped from one danger only to fall into a greater one...

Aristophanes holds in his greedy and criminal hands an undeniable power of decision over the life or death of anyone. As an avowed member of the Court of the Holy Office, he acts supported and covered by authorities who are "above good and evil", in the most varied departments of the State.

– What are you doing here, man? – He asks Wladimir directly –. Did you lose your tongue by any chance? If it were missing, it would save you from a lot of embarrassment and sleeplessness! But everything has its time!

Wladimir feels a shiver run down his spine. Cautious, he considers what he will say:

– Sir, we were just walking by, when the soldiers stopped us, suspecting we don't know what! Helpless, we could do nothing, they simply acted violently! Confident in heavenly powers, which would surely save us from the worst, if that were God's supreme will, we simply obeyed!

Aristophanes caresses his well-groomed beard as he thinks.

He hates the man for all he stands for, but if he tries to accuse or penalize him in any way, he will dangerously challenge some prominent figures in Florence, and for the moment he has other more important and urgent matters.

Being a man of authority and power, Aristophanes is aware that Wladimir is very cautious. He has long known his wisdom, his power of oratory and persuasion. The latter, who at that moment is facing a brutal reality, is one of the most powerful and respected intelligences in Florence.

Using his prerogatives, he arrogantly declares:

– You know how much I dislike your presence and your usual disgrace! However, I see nothing here that can incriminate a man like you! I know your faith, behavior and character!
Don't think of this as a compliment, but only as an observation, one of those that intelligence compels us to make! We are not really kind to each other, but here and now I can decide life or death for you! I know you are not ignorant of my power!

Internally, in spite of the gravity of the moment, Wladimir cannot avoid a clear and just thought:

Only God can decide, in fact, the life or death of anyone, including yours, weak and defenseless man...!"

In the light of Wladimir's cautious silence and intuiting his intelligent reflections, Aristophanes orders the imposition:

– Get out of here! Thank good fortune for allowing me to be the judge of your case! Otherwise, the heaven you love so much would be honored to welcome you before your time.

Without arguing, Wladimir waits respectfully as he makes a small bow.

With the matter resolved, Aristophanes pulls the luxurious reins of his horse, twists them to the side and intends to ride off, when he hears Wladimir's kind and polite voice:

– Thank you in the name of heaven! For me and my son!

Looking at them indifferently, he presses the spurs, which causes the horse to rear up dangerously before leaving. Aristophanes enjoys the powerful effects he has wherever he goes.

In a few moments, he disappears with his entourage.

And as he leaves, taking with him the sleeping body of the one who started these sad events and who even unintentionally allowed everything to be resolved, finally freeing them from certain death, Wladimir and Norbert throw themselves into each other's arms and burst into tears...

Trembling and very dejected, they kneel down on the stones of the street and raise a silent prayer of gratitude to God. They would never forget that terrible day...!

After this terrifying experience, father and son, traumatized, took some time to recover and resume their lives... Almost at the same time, both come back to reality.

Still under painful feelings, Wladimir asks:

– Were we both immersed in the same memories, son?

– It seems so...

– We learned a lot in a few hours! We certainly needed that lesson.

– Fortunately, it was not yet our time to leave this world!

– On that almost fateful day, despite the sad prognosis, we survived! You were so small, my son, and I had so many plans!

– These memories coincide with what we have been feeling these past few days! What do you intend to do with the diatribes of those who do anything to harm us? We sail daily in a dark and treacherous sea! And woe to those who challenge the laws created and maintained by a dubious, inhuman and deeply arbitrary power! In the face of these powerful people, we are always *personae non gratae*, therefore, with an uncertain future. They do not even hide their unbridled impulse to attack us!

Norbert takes a deep breath, then pauses and continues:

– It is with great effort that I manage to control myself from reacting to their constant offenses, challenges and traps! I feel like unmasking them! However, I know that this would lead to us being taken to jail, victims of their abominable tortures, and then to the gallows or to the crackling bonfires; or even to both practices, concomitantly...!

Wladimir sighs and nods:

– We know very well the path we are walking on... with our feet and hands tied, we are surprised by a gigantic monster with its open jaws, ready to swallow those who dare to defy it. These men, if we can still define them as such, sabotage attempts of progress on the face of this planet, especially today, in Florence and similar cities, which are great places of knowledge and immeasurable potential for the future.

Norbert asks:

– How much longer are we going to be forced to live a life of surrender to god Moloch?!

Touched, he exposes his righteous disgust.

As a father and companion in profession, struggles and ideals, Wladimir admires him with pride. However, he fears losing him...

His son carries the strength of courage and passion in his blood and soul. Norbert reflects the radiant aura of great men, advocate of good and truth, above all circumstances, to establish true justice in the world.

Wladimir once again brings both hands to his tight chest...

Norbert calms down and observes his emotion. He embraces him with respect and full of love, while gently apologizing:

– Forgive me, father! Everything will be alright!

– Certainly, son! Empowered by those who are by our side, we will continue!

Norbert nods. Smiling, Wladimir tries to relax:

– Am I wrong or are you in love?

Norbert is delighted by his father's admirable ability to read into his soul like an open book.

Enigmatic, he admires a beautiful tiny bird flying.

– And so? – Insists his father. Laughing likewise, he replies:

– And what is new?

– I am talking about a deeper feeling, my son! The one that puts the sparkle of the stars in your eyes!

In fact, Wladimir knows his son.

Looking at his father with tenderness, he responded moved:

– I neither confirm nor deny it, for now! Wait and see ...!

Touching him lightly on the shoulder and bidding him farewell, Wladimir goes, leaving him to his reveries of a philosopher and dreamer even though he is also very rational and practical.

Wladimir loves his son with all his soul and will do anything for him. He educated him in fervent submission to the heavenly powers. An easy task, since Norbert from birth already carried in the depths of his luminous soul the eternal truths, surprisingly detached from the contradictions and prejudices of the world.

Without extremism, Norbert is a man of great faith.

It reminds him of his mother, his beloved Isolde, pious and kind, who would make any man happy. However, she had always revealed that she did not belong to the world. Luminous, she passed like a benevolent comet and brought his son, a rare gift from heaven.

He never forgot her and never replaced her, neither in his heart nor in his life.

This way of living and being, however, sometimes brings him a deep loneliness.

If it were not for the company of his son and the spontaneous joys of the soul...

Passionate about life, he loves everything it offers. The simplest things awaken in him a great charm. Reverential, humble and conscientious, nature. The more your immersion in the sciences, the more you will be enchanted by the laws that govern and command everything in an admirable perfection.

Wladimir only rests when his exhausted body forces him to do so. There is much to do and time is short.

In an exhausting vigilance, it is necessary to be alert to everything and everyone in order to survive with dignity and in relative safety; to take care of the aspects of matter and those related to the spirit; to remember the past and the good lessons it taught us, while watching over the present and building the future, not only for himself, but for the world as a whole, with the aim of fulfilling his human aspirations, as a citizen of a world in the process of intellectual and moral improvement.

2.– PANDERVA

Wrapped in rags, terrified, a young woman, almost a child, runs wildly through the streets of the city. In her eyes, an expression of terror. Turning to look behind, from time to time, she confirms the presence of a presumed pursuer, so she takes shortcuts through alleys, over bridges, across streams, up and down hills.

Sweating heavily, she runs relentlessly.

Who is she, where did she come from, from what or from whom is she escaping so desperately?

The miserable, those who live for God, know her. Her name is Panderva.

With no whereabouts, she wanders the streets of Florence.

But, after all, who is chasing her? Who is Panderva so afraid of?

Looking around, we see nothing and no matter how hard we try, everything remains the same.

From whom is this mortal of exuberant beauty escaping in such anguish, affected by needs of all kinds and dressed in rags that barely cover her body...?

Her enemies, at this moment, hidden to us, may be flesh and blood, so dangerous. Perhaps it is someone seeking to have fun at her expense, or some violent man with the vile criminal intention of subduing her.

After a few hours, exhausted, she hides in a dark alley.

Exhausted, she huddles, moans and murmurs prayers while observing her surroundings with glassy eyes.

She shudders at any sound, whether from the wind, or from some other unfortunate, as lost as she is, or even from the animals wandering about looking for something to relieve their overwhelming hunger.

In this place, of bad appearance and reputation, very few venture out, except the disinherited of fortune who crowd in and share their prevailing misery.

Little by little, Panderva lets her body fall loosely to the ground, gets more comfortable and closes her eyes. A benevolent drowsiness sweetly envelops her.

A scrawny little dog that seems to know her approaches, wags its tail and begins to lick her face and arms. Trembling, she defends herself, but despite her extreme fatigue, she knows who is caressing her.

Panderva smiles and in this happy smile we can see the "face" of the Creator.

A few hours have passed, when she finally wakes up.

She looks around, surprises the little animal and exclaims with affection:

– Hello, my little friend! You must be hungry! You are always hungry! I have food in my bag, take it!

Said and done, she gives him a piece of dark, greasy and somewhat dirty meat she had found on the road.

Wagging his tail frenetically and his bright eyes showing his gratitude, the little animal receives the food and eats greedily.

Opening her big, luminous eyes, she contemplates with pleasure the voracity of her friend.

She still looks around, frightened...

Finally, she is ready to walk. This time she has company.

A few more minutes pass and she decides on the route. So, with light steps, she walks through streets she already knows without stopping.

Her expression now is no longer one of fear, but of pleasant anticipation.

After a while, she sees an elegant street full of beautiful mansions.

The wealthy and well-dressed people passing by drive her away because they fear her.

Ignoring them blatantly, she continues on her way while rehearsing some dance steps.

The skeletal animal runs and barks loudly. Panderva looks at the different houses and sees the beautiful and rich one that interests her, the objective of her journey.

She takes a deep breath and heads there.

She pauses for a moment to smooth her tunic, straighten her hair as beautiful as ripe wheat, dirty and tangled, and brush the hem oh her skirt. Finally, with her lush pink cheeks, she smiles satisfied with the result.

She circles the building and climbs the back stairs. She is known and always welcomed in this house.

Playful, delicate and smiling, she approaches with light steps, as if she were floating.

Someone very special occupies her thoughts: a good man smiles at her as he calls her "dear friend." Imagine! She, someone's friend? "How good is this son of God...!" – She thinks, slowing down and organizing her thoughts and intentions.

Her proclaimed "madness" drives most people away from her. Some even run away from her, as if she has some contagious disease.

Sometimes they have fun at her expense.

On these occasions, satisfied to be the object of attention, she accepts their provocations; though sometimes, while they are laughing out loud, they go so far as to hurt her. Nevertheless, she resists steadfastly.

She suffers without moaning or complaining! After all, what would they think? That she's a fool, who does not know how to have fun?!

Panderva thinks her own name is very strange, but she has learned to like it, and when the good man pronounces it, it is prettier! Finally, checking her appearance once more, she knocks on the big oak door.

A strong old man opens it and, recognizing her, cannot hide some discomfort.

Panderva is disappointed... After all, she had dressed so nicely and even cleaned her face!

Finally, resigned to her visit and respecting the wishes of his boss, whom he likes very much, Cyrene orders:

– Come in, come in! We always have some food – Already in a different mood, he smiles and, with the intention of provoking her, suggests:

– You can also take a shower and change these rags!

Annoyed, she replies:

– I can accept the clothes, Cyrene, but the bath, no and no...!

Continuing with the conversation, Cyrene says:

– Well, well, Forbes will be happy to help you! – He cackles with amused laughter.

Panderva grimaces and steps back as she vents:

– God help me from that Forbes! She scrubs me so hard with the brush and soap that my skin almost peels off! After the shower I get redder than a ripe bell pepper!

She finishes her sentence by crossing her arms as she stomps her little foot on the floor and stubbornly looks down.

Laughing, Cyrene analyzes how beautiful this little creature is. And how she knows how to defend herself!

He shakes his arms and nods:

– All right! All right...! First food, then, who knows, right?

She remains silent and frowning.

Cyrene then plays his best cards. He has known this game for a long time:

– Think about it, if the boss arrives and you are still here, he will be delighted to see you clean and well-dressed!

Swaying back and forth, and easing her expression, she replies:

– Well... Who knows, right...? – A little discouraged, she asks:

– So, the good man is not at home?

Cyrene shakes his head, confirming the absence of his boss.

– Ah... Well, well, I wasted my time! And I came from so far away!

– Maybe not.. – The man answers her, already sorry for her disillusionment.

Cyrene enters the house. He has been working there for many years.

After a few minutes, he returns with a large tray with a steaming bowl of soup, fruits and sweets. Sitting on the floor, she takes the food and expresses her gratitude.

With a wooden spoon, she greedily eats the delicious food.

The soup contains large pieces of meat that she eats with delight. At the same time, she keeps small portions in her grimy bag. Satisfied, she finally finishes the tasty meal.

Taking a break, she reverently admires the beauty of the fruits before eating them and reflects on how good Cyrene is.

She looks at him sadly when she realizes he is getting old. Knowing that he will soon die, she feels very sorry for him.

After such a hearty meal, which she can rarely afford, she gets comfortable as best she can, and in a few moments falls asleep.

With her hands and arms supporting her face, Panderva breathes softly and serenely...

She is already used to sleeping like this, anywhere. There are no difficulties she cannot overcome.

On her almost childish and very beautiful face, there is a slight smile of satisfaction.

Cyrene shakes his head and refuses to approach her. If he offers her another place to rest, she will not accept.

Quite often, Panderva declares that she does not deserve this or that... Does not she deserve it...? Cyrene finds it very strange...

"Anyway, crazy people and children must be understood and it is not always possible to question them!" – He learned that from the beginning.

Admiring her beauty, Cyrene thinks that an angel should live in that perfect body.

"A body tormented by a sick mind. Ah, the mysteries of God...!" – he concludes.

He leaves her alone and goes back to his business. The bosses are very demanding, despite being fair and generous.

In the street, the little dog had fallen asleep hiding in a corner, under a stone staircase, at the entrance of the huge house.

✱ ✱ ✱

Taking advantage of our attributions as author and readers, let us investigate the life and reasons for the existence of this peculiar character. How many times have we ventured down these roads and sometimes, to the horror or delight of our hearts, we have found ourselves...?

That is because we write, untiringly, out of habit or pleasure – or more appropriately out of spiritual necessity –, stories of lives seemingly forgotten in space and time.

One day, we will only be able to write beautiful stories, full of wonderful examples!

After all, progress drives us onwards and upwards, irresistibly! It is of the Law!

One day, our dear Panderva had everything the world could offer and it was too much for her.

She was not a bad person; however, she eventually succumbed under the fascination of wealth and power.

After living a childhood and youth far from problems and worries, she faced what her royal position demanded of her. With the death of her father, the king, she became queen, but being unprepared for this task, she settled in, without assuming her royal duties as she should have.

At that time, she achieved the realization of her dreams as a woman, marrying her favorite, deceived; however, her feelings, elevated to the highest degree of wealth and human prominence, led to enjoy a luxurious and pleasurable existence.

Life; however, which surprises us at every moment, changed the plans of the young and beautiful queen, leaving her in bed, victim of a mysterious and incurable disease. Discouraged by the doctors of the kingdom, she got worse and worse.

From her comfortable and luxurious bed, she quickly watched her husband leave, bored and indifferent to her sufferings.

Gradually he lost his scruples and, making use of his powers, began to spend a lot of money on those who could accompany him in his madness, often replacing them with others and others, spending his time in multiple absurdities.

Sick, his queen was a sad spectacle whom he avoided, forgetting her more and more.

As she convulsed in pain between the silk sheets stained by her sores, this queen, now dethroned, anxiously longed for more time in her life to change.

It was already too late for her; however, when she surrendered her soul to the Creator amidst the rites of her religion, which she despised even in her last days out of servility and interest, she witnessed infinite glories and joys in the kingdom of Heaven and the warm reception of angels.

After her death she was shocked by the consequences of a life of blatant errors. She had been a woman magnetized, by affinity, towards her accomplices. Many had left the world amidst pain, tears, hunger, thirst and disease because of her.

After a long period of tragic wandering, she finally ambushed herself in the flesh and was reborn. However, rejected by the one who granted her life, she was abandoned.

Her mother, enemy of the past, who had attracted her presence without love and responsibility, had ordered a trusted servant to put an end to the little burden.

So, the newborn Panderva cried stridently in a dark and lonely place.

Some passersby saw her, wrinkled their noses and moved on, concluding that the event was none of their business.

After a few minutes, a dog approached her. Alone and despised, equally hungry and cold, he lay down beside her, warming himself and warming her.

A few minutes later, a drunken man passing by noticed them both.

Putting aside the empty bottle, he struggled to understand what he was seeing. emotional due to the excesses of alcohol, he observed this helpless little creature.

He leaned over her and, stumbling, trying hard not to fall, he managed to take her in his arms while mumbling incomprehensible words. He held her tightly, straightened up as best he could and zigzagged through the streets, still not knowing what to do about it.

After a long walk, with extreme difficulty, he saw an acquaintance as misfit as himself.

Almost collapsing and feeling the urgent need to surrender to sleep, he looked at her in silence, showing her the little creature. At the surprise stamped on the "friend's face", and before she could refuse the "commission", he handed her the baby and left, without further ado, disappearing into the corners of the alleys.

The woman, grimacing disapprovingly, looked at the child, not knowing what to do with her.

Perhaps it would be better to leave it there... A few moments later, she began to think:

"With many tears, some whimpers, painful moans, and this burden in my arms I will be able to sensitize passers-by and earn more money!"

From then on, in the most miserable way imaginable, Panderva grew up in the midst of abuse and constant hunger.

After the sufferings of her fatal illness, she had prayed in spirituality for a chance of redemption, in a life completely opposite to the one she had.

Time passed and one day Minerva – this is the name of her adoptive "mother" – ordered her to steal and prostitute herself.

Refusing, Panderva was brutally beaten.

With tears of pain, disillusionment and rebellion, she decided to flee far away, and at the first opportunity she fulfilled her intention. Thus, she ventured on unknown roads and spent many days like this, keeping her distance from Minerva.

Accustomed to living on the streets, Panderva performed small jobs in exchange for a few coins.

Physically strong, she blossomed into a beautiful flower. Eccentric in her way of being, haughty despite the rags she wears, of easy speech and indisputable good taste, she feels very comfortable, in the midst of the luxury and refinement of nobility.

She is called crazy, but she has learned not to care about other people's opinions and continues her itinerant and miserable life.

Apart from the great difficulties she faces every day, she loves people and helps those she meets along the way.

She devotes immense love to animals, respecting their fragility and innocence.

With an extraordinary beauty that poverty cannot hide, she evokes sympathy, but faces great risks from rough and violent men who try to dominate her, aiming to satiate their brutal appetites.

On these occasions, they are astonished by her reaction and defensive power, as well as by the providential circumstances that saved her from the worst.

Panderva also suffers persecutions and attacks by sinister figures, which, although imponderable, exhibit terrifying and almost concrete forms.

When Cyrene returns to the kitchen, she is still asleep. He respects her rest, which he considers sacred, and leaves quietly.

On his way out, he encounters Forbes, who is heading to the kitchen, humming something high-pitched. He signals to her and points to the girl. Forbes grimaces as she comments sullenly:

– Here comes extra work! This girl knows how to piss me off! A naughty elf couldn't be more demonic! And when you feel threatened? Oh, oh, oh, oh...! She's a wild child!

– Only with you, Forbes! She defends herself against your authority so, so... shall we say, so, so, imposing!

– She needs someone to curb her temper. Ah! Just today when rheumatism attacked me. There's no part of my body that isn't suffering! – She mutters as she walks away, dragging her feet.

Meanwhile, Panderva dreams that she is a beautiful and powerful princess... Her palace is of unimaginable beauty, with servants looking after her comfort and safety; after all, her father is a very demanding king... A bit... Cruel, perhaps...

How good it is to live like this...! To have everything anyone could wish for!

Beautiful men live at her feet, but her heart already belongs to the handsome and brave Genebaldo...! If he didn't exist, all she is and has would be worthless...!

Panderva remains immersed in her dreams...

Meanwhile, the owner of the house arrives, gets rid of his luggage, his coat, his gloves and puts his hat on a small hanger in the hallway.

Cyrene greets him with bows and smiles, sincere and spontaneous.

Wladimir thanks him for his kind reception, as he reflects on the difficulties Cyrene would surely face if he were not there. One day he defended this good man from a fault he had not committed, ultimately setting him free, only to discover that he was not from Florence and was just passing through.

Cyrene had no destination and no safe landing. His life was then similar to his own, in the past, when he struggled fiercely to survive.

He took an interest in him and discovered that in Genoa he had been a skilled manager.

Knowing that Cyrene wished to stay here and seeing in him someone worthy of great trust, he offered him the role of manager of his house. If he found something more interesting, he could leave whenever he wanted.

Cyrene thanked him effusively for the opportunity to solve his problems and gladly accepted. Working in Wladimir's house, he didn't even notice the time passing. He stayed and cleaved to his boss and his son Norbert. Today, Wladimir would no longer give up this good and faithful servant.

Cyrene makes a daily effort to ensure that everything runs successfully.

In everyday life, he became more and more indispensable, besides having won their hearts completely.

– Hello, Cyrene! – Wladimir exclaims, grateful for the opportunity to have crossed the path of this upright and fraternal man.

After receiving him, Cyrene declares:

– I will never get tired of thanking you for everything, my lord! At that moment I was lost and could not defend myself! Desperate for the loss of my only son, I just wanted to die! I don't know how I fell into that trap so well set by the devil...! But if it was him, "the spell turned against the sorcerer", because after all that happened, I had the joy of coming to work in this house!

– Don't blaspheme, Cyrene! Only God could have brought you to us! Today, you are part of this house and of our lives!

– Count on me always! – he declares reverently.

– Thank you! Thank you! And so? Is everything all right?

– Yes! It is! I would like to show you something!

Smiling slightly, Wladimir comments:

– I can even imagine what it is!

The two head for the spacious and comfortable kitchen.

There he sees the girl lying on the floor sleeping very comfortably and smiling tenderly, so carelessly, confidently and fragilely.

Speaking quietly, Cyrene tells him when she arrived and that she had been waiting for him.

– Let me know when she wakes up. I conclude that this is the natural reaction to a substantial meal.

– That's right, my lord! You know how it is, don't you? She lives as she pleases, without eating well. When you eat well...

Wladimir takes distance, because as his good servant, he knows Panderva's eccentric habits and unusual reactions.

He is very fond of her and would like to protect her if she would consent, but in her recklessness and naivety, she does not even imagine the risks she runs, even when she faces them and gets hurt, as had happened to him, so many times.

As he walks away, he thinks of his dear son who at this hour must be holding his office at the Provincial Court.

"Who will inhabit his dreams of young man...?" – He thinks.

Norbert is fiercely desired by women. Either for his beauty, elegance and distinction, or for his noble character, or even for the important position he holds with the powerful.

After a comforting bath, Wladimir, dressed in more practical and comfortable clothes, goes to the library and there, while consulting some scientific works, he mentally goes over what at this moment causes him fear and much uncertainty about the future.

Those who live in that era cannot ignore the cruel and cleverly placed traps under the feet of those who are at the top or on their way to desired glories.

It is impossible to be part of a city like Florence, to reach high positions and not be subject to persecution.

The vision of vultures devouring lives and fortunes falls singularly on those who, possessing titles and the approval of good people, own considerable wealth. And this is his case...

He seems to walk in a rotten and treacherous swamp.

Without colluding with the "powerful" who orbit around current, dishonest, venal, and hypocritical authorities, nor with their retrogressive ideas - so well accepted by the dogmatic and tyrannical clergy that arms them to achieve their goals - he and

Norbert are closely watched and "marked" to be removed from the path of those who, crazily and ambitiously, seek to seize the realms of heaven and earth.

And woe to those who do not move at the same pace and dare to confront them, challenging their false sanctities... Woe to those who follow the paths of dignity and honor and do not bow down before them!

Wladimir suffers twice: for himself and for Norbert, who, like him, acts prudently, but with a big heart.

Father and son use the laws, invariably subjecting them to divine power, for which they would die.

So they live on a tightrope hanging over an abyss. How long will they be able to keep this rope taut and secure?

Today, Vladimir went to the appropriate departments to listen and understand what is happening, trying by all means to explain his point of view. However, he encountered a stone wall, insensitive and cold, indifferent to anything but earthly glory and power.

If in fact there are political and religious confrontations, they will only have the defense and protection of the Creator.

One of the painful aspects of this conflict is his scientific thesis.

There is freedom to delve into subjects in various academies and even to conduct experiments, as long as results are consecrated in full confirmation of the laws of the Church, since any other idea, even if rationally proven, must necessarily conform to its dictates.

Wladimir shudders at the sinister spectacles that the town witnesses when the regime acts with cruelty and refinement.

However, in spite of this, Wladimir, his son and others stand up undaunted against this situation.

He takes a deep breath and concludes that waking up in relative peace and being able to go to work every morning is already a great blessing.

He prays fervently that he will not be swallowed up by this infectious sinkhole that smells like sulfur...

pretending sainthood, despite the abominable acts they practice, civil and ecclesiastical personalities are venerated and disliked wherever they go, like rare birds of beautiful plumage, exotic and arrogant.

The slavish submission of people reaches unimaginable levels, after all, challenging the current power can result in imprisonment, torture, accusation of heresy and finally cruel death. For this reason, they keep silence.

When man commits crimes, because he is under protection, he invests in the creation of a deformed world, suited to his evil tendencies.

Upon his return, Wladimir felt worse than before.

Spirits are very high, which raises suspicions of well-defined plans for the destiny and future of Florence.

He and his son, as well as his companions, are closely watched and their enemies are already anticipating the pleasure of destroying them...

This beautiful and flourishing city, as well as Genoa, Venice and others with similar potential, have a reserved place in history. That is why they are infested with wolves.

Focusing his reflections on a more subtle level, Wladimir analyzes, lucidly and intuitively, the actions of the shadows that take advantage of their earthly representatives.

Those who dominate are almost always manipulated by malevolent entities that, absorbing their vital energies, control their life to use them in dark harmonies.

In the clash of forces between good and evil, the extraphysical world provides constituent elements to attract, strengthen and decide, since the results will always depend on the free will of those who make decisions.

But, above all, even though it may appear incomprehensible to ordinary people, the great Law is fulfilled.

Completely absorbed, Wladimir shudders when he hears the voice of Cyrene:

– Sir, Panderva has already woken up, she repeated the same old scenes with poor Forbes and is finally ready to see you!

Smiling complacently, he also makes an observation:

– This clean and well-dressed girl really impresses! Elegant and proud as she is, she would be all the rage in court! And I have no doubt, sir, she would captivate many a heart...!

– I agree with you, Cyrene; however, may God keep her away from that world of traps so dangerous to naive hearts like that of this good daughter of God!

– You are right... It would be like throwing a little sheep to the wolves...!

– You understand me, Cyrene! Whenever you want, you can bring her!

In spite of his mood, Wladimir needs to listen to her.

Panderva, like so many others who live according to God, is persecuted and despised. On top of that, he holds her in high steem.

Despite her character, she expresses herself very well and has very advanced ideas.

In his house, she ended up winning everyone's heart. Even Forbes treats her with severity, as she would do with a beloved daughter.

With her naive naturalness and the bravery with which she faces "the dragons of life," Panderva is admirable.

Though dressed in rags and wandering hither and thither, sleeping in the streets and dark alleys, without rest or shelter, she reveals a beautiful soul.

Within minutes, Panderva appears at the entrance, respectful and hesitant.

– Come in, dear friend! – He says, encouraging her fraternally.

Shy but very pleased with what she has just heard, she remains silent. She is the one who always has a good answer on the tip of her tongue!

This kind man; however, charms her, awakening an unwavering affection and trust in her.

Not even among those with whom she breaks bread had she ever encountered such kindness!

In silence, she continues to stare at this man, who, in spite of awakening so many good feelings in her soul, intimidates her too much.

– So, Panderva? You wanted to see me?

– Yes! Whenever I come here, I want to see you and I am very disappointed when you are not at home...!

– Panderva! When I am away, wait for me! If I am on a trip, Cyrene will let you know! Anyway, why did you want to talk to me?

While smiling at her spontaneity, Wladimir sits her down on a chair.

Panderva takes a deep breath and reflects on what she is about to say and, almost regretfully, declares:

– I apologize! It's not worth wasting time with me!

– Now, why do you say that? I take care of my time; besides I like talking to you! Tell me, what do you want?

She organizes her thoughts and replies:

– It's been a while; I have got a lot going on in my head!

– Well, it happens to all of us, believe it!

– It's true, but what I have in my mind must be very different from what you have...!

Wladimir does not resist and laughs heartily.

Laughing too, she continues:

– I would like to know who I am and where I come from! It is hard to live like this... I do not have a proper name...!

– I see... And what do you expect from me, Panderva?

– I tell you, good man! You and your son Norbert understand a lot about law and could help me, because I do not know what to do!

– You are right... However, do not get your hopes up, because despite legal resources, situations like yours are difficult to resolve. It may be that there are no records...

– I understand... I am just a drop of water in this ocean of people with no identity! However, kind man, God is with you and your son!

Wladimir admires her ability to formulate thoughts and explain herself:

– We are grateful, good friend! He always grants us what is best for us!

– I do believe it! I want to tell you that for me your home is a unique and incomparable place! – She smiles playfully and adds: – The one who does not like to see me here is Forbes...

Although Wladimir understands the girl's way of being, he says:

– Please, Panderva! Think about it a little and be more tolerant! Forbes is only doing it for your own good!

– Why does she give so many orders?

– To organize our house well, Panderva. And you rise up against her care!

– That's because when she yells at me, I cannot control myself! You must understand, good man, I am not used to it!

Thinking about Forbes, Wladimir explains somewhat worried:

– Forbes is sick, Panderva. I already tried to hire someone else to help her, but she does not accept. She declares that she can handle everything and does not need anyone else! Anyway, she really likes to work!

– She really likes to give orders! – Panderva insists. Wladimir smiles and gives up:

– Well, let's forget about these matters! I promise to investigate your past and origins, okay?

– Yes, I thank you very much!

– As for your uncertain and itinerant life, we have already offered you a great solution...!

Panderva sighs and says:

– Aren't you afraid of living with a lunatic?

– Do not say that, Panderva! We know that is not true!

– How can you know if I have doubts myself?!

– Why, Panderva? – Saddened, she confesses:

– Because I see things that no one sees, I hear voices when no one is talking, and sometimes I change so much that I do not even recognize myself! I say things I do not mean and do actions that surprise everyone! I foresee events that will happen and know things that I was never taught! Oh, good man, and so many other things!

She is already on the verge of tears. Wladimir asks:

– Calm down, Panderva! Do not be like that! Despite everything you say, it is impossible to see malice or madness in you...! These events are reactions of the soul, human potentials often difficult to analyze satisfactorily! I would love to be able to help you find yourself, but for that it would be necessary to have you around. Why don't you accept to live in my house? Forbes would take good care of you and you would have everything you need; you would be more protected here and we could analyze your behavior and try to help you!

– Living with Forbes? God help me! She is terrible! She talks nonstop and complains about everything! And when she decides that I must obey her, then it becomes difficult, good man...!

Wladimir smiles and thinks how much she is unknowingly helping him to relax and ease his own heart a little.

– Her methods are a bit rough, but her intention is good, believe me!

– I do not need to be taken care of! I have always done it myself! – she insists.

– However, my dear friend, you live in the midst of dangers of all kinds...!

– It is the price I pay for my freedom, why?

– Freedom requires responsibility!

– Am I not responsible? – The question sounded like a complaint.

– Do you know how many people see you and harass you because of your weirdness! This is very dangerous!

To continue living like this is unacceptable. When living amidst danger, hunger, cold and uncertainty, you are unable to think better of yourself.

Listening to him, very attentive at first, Panderva stands up in ecstasy. Her gaze becomes brighter and she begins to speak. Her voice seems to come from far away, though it sounds vibrant and pleasant:

– You and your son face difficult problems! Both of you are in great danger...! I see men who are shadows and shadows who are men...! They are very evil...! They live because they plot your loss and the ruin of your house!

Beware! Evil will come and both will need much vigilance and divine protection to defeat it...! Never; however, lose faith in who truly carries our destiny in his hands...! The superior lights illuminate and protect you! We, your protectors, will be attentive and we will do everything possible, so that you continue your journey of science, justice and love...! Peace and light to your heart, friend, brother...!

Proudly, Panderva approaches Wladimir, blessing him... Then she slowly steps back and automatically lowers her arms.

Like a sleepwalker, she goes back to her seat and collapses there. She looks around and asks:

– What did I say? Why are you looking at me like that? I see tears in your eyes, good man. Did I do something to hurt you? Forgive me...! Didn't I tell you? I am a hopeless wanderer! I will never be able to get better! I do not even deserve your attention...!

The last sentence sounded so sad that Wladimir felt deeply sorry.

Still digesting everything he heard about his and his son's fate, he felt moved and wanted to thank her for what she said. Panderva was God's instrument to help them.

So, Wladimir said to her:

– Do not say that, my daughter! You are a blessed oracle! But be careful never to act like that in front of people who could do you a lot of harm...! Do you know what they do to people like you, Panderva?

– Yes, I do... I have seen horrible things! People dying at the hands of executioners and claiming their innocence, poor things!

– Tortures are carried out in secret, but executions are carried out in broad daylight, in intimidating spectacles... So don't do what you just did, okay? For your safety!

– How not to do it? I never know when it will happen! Something very strong dominates me...!

– To evaluate your peculiar behavior, my dear friend, you must think about my invitation!

Shaking her head, she makes it clear that she is going to think about it. So, Wladimir concludes:

– I pray God to bless you and protect you always...!

– May it be so! – She answers, bowing her head reverently.

– Well, Panderva, I have other things to do for now. Come back another day and we will talk more, okay?

– Yes, see you soon!

– See you soon, Panderva!

Wladimir understands that he owes more attention and care to this creature of God. And he will also have to devote more time to help her clarify her doubts.

He waits for his son's arrival so that he can talk about what happened:

– "I thank the one who alerted me and blessed me in the name of God!

This confirms my fears, but assures me that, if we act according to the laws of the Lord and are attentive, we can be saved from the storm that is coming..."

Now, he and Norbert will need more than ever to be vigilant and pray, as well as observe and look for traps...

Who to trust? How to defend oneself? Against the evil that is attached to the laws created and exercised by the tyrants of the world, there is no way to defend oneself...!

He goes to the house chapel and there he bows and prays for a long time. Exhausted, he cannot hold back his tears.

He aspires with all his heart for a better world... Who knows if one day it will come true?... If not because of him, it will be because of those who come after him! Though the centuries may bend upon themselves, someday life will be better, because men through sufferings will have learned that evil is treacherous and affects all those who are in tune with it. With great difficulty, all will learn, at last, the messages of the divine Lamb!

If he and his son, like so many others, serve as a foundation for building this new and redeemed world, so be it! This will have been a glorious way to live and die! "We are all immersed in this immeasurable Universe, so vast and so beautiful! In the grandiose vision of the heavens on a starry night, how many points of light send us messages that must be glorious! How many spaces of learning and living!

What beauty and perfection!

"Oh, Almighty God, bless our lives and our destinies! Protect us from evil and lead us in the paths of good and love...! I submit to your love and power, always! Do with me, Father, as you wish...!"

Thus, Wladimir ends his prayers and finally finds the serenity of the righteous of good souls and clear consciences...

3.– THE COURT AND THE NOBLEMAN

When Panderva, beautifully dressed – thanks to Forbes' strenuous work – left Wladimir's house, she looked for the little dog sleeping under the stairs.

Sensing her footsteps and her presence, he awoke from his sleep and ran to her, wagging his tail.

Panderva sat down on a stair and offered him the generous portions of meat she had kept in her bag.

She smiled at the sight of him desperate with so much food. He didn't know what to attack first. He was chomping on this and that until he was full.

"Days and days without eating properly, poor thing…" – She thinks, forgetting that she lives like that too.

She calls the little animal who begins to hop happily as they walk away.

Singing, she exudes the joy of having been heard and welcomed.

Wladimir's house has become an oasis for Panderva, where she finds respect, affection and security. To Know that they are there and that she can count on them is truly providential.

"There, I feel protected, but submitting to Forbes' orders? Agrr! However, I have to think about it… The good man promised to help me find out who I am and he always keeps what he promises...!" – She reflects.

Still focused on her reflections, she hears some chanting.

The songs are sacred; the rhythm is monotonous and dreary... The voices are shrill and discordant...

Guessing the reasons for all the commotion, she feels her heart beating wildly.

A strange physical weakness takes hold of her. She leans against a wall, feeling an unbearable anguish.

It all portends something terrible...! She shudders and suddenly feels very cold...

In panic, she sees a procession preceded by banners with figures of saints, religious leaders in their taller robes.

Trembling in terror, Panderva looks at their heavy, hardened features, and thinks:

– "whoever does this can only be bad, very bad...!" – She concludes.

The noisy and somber procession runs through the street in the display of its colors, rhythms and its representative figures, confirming a grotesque and criminal reality.

Colored ribbons and serpentines are waving on the banners; some of them are as black as mourning...!

People abandon their occupations, their comfortable homes, the alleys or the wells where they survive and more and more crowd together.

On some faces, Panderva can see devilish expressions with a morbid expectation for what they see and for what they already anticipate, sadists...

She observes a decorated wagon in the street, and inside there is a scrawny woman with her hair loose and tied with ropes.

People around her shout offensive words and insult God, cursing her.

Some throw stones, fruit peels and other trash at her.

She reacts weakly, trying to dodge them without achieving her intention.

Her clothes are long and dark-colored. At her waist, ropes tighten around her coarse and loose garments.

With glassy eyes, she anxiously searches among the crowd for a friendly face.

Trying to touch hearts, she shouts at the top of her lungs:

– Mercy, for God's sake! I am innocent! I cannot be condemned! I have little children to raise! Have mercy on me, men of God, and free me from such a cruel fate... Oh, let me return to the arms of my children...! – She pleads with a hoarse voice to the religious who are there, but who turn a deaf ear to her desperate pleas, raising the sound of their voices, intoning the endless plainchant.

Maddened, the woman struggles, looks up and begs heaven to protect her.

A small group of people cry and struggle to keep up with the vehicle.

Panderva assumes they are her desperate family and friends in the face of such horror...

– "Poor unfortunate ones! How much pain...!"– She thinks, while her legs tremble.

Impossible not to remember Wladimir's advice... She herself may someday go through a terrible experience...! Is this woman as rare as she is...?

"And how many more, my lord?" – She thinks with horror.

The wheels of the wagon creaked, harmonizing with the pain and weeping of the condemned woman.

In the midst of this paraphernalia, the little dog looks at Panderva and whimpers in evident distress.

She puts him on her lap and hugs him:

– Calm down, little friend! I am here... Be quiet... Come on, let's get out of here...

With tears welling up in her beautiful eyes, she says almost to herself:

– These malicious people arrest, torture, condemn and execute people who have forgotten the divine law that says: "Thou shalt not kill...!" They claim to be God's representatives, but they do not do His will...!

Panderva cannot stand it any longer and lets her tears flow. She cries for this unhappy woman, for all those who once were or will be equally unfortunate, for herself and for all the evil that exists in the world.

As the procession, that looks like a nightmare, moves away, she tries to warm up the little dog, who is still shivering.

Suddenly, she hears:

– Do you know that poor woman?

Panderva turns and sees the beautiful eyes of a nobleman, dressed with all the details of his social class; feathered hat in one hand; long, black, shiny boots, wrapped in a range of pleasant perfumes.

She feels strange in front of him... She looks at him as if she were in a dream or a nightmare.

His presence gives her a mixture of joy and deep disgust. Without understanding, she takes a deep breath and answers:

– No, but I know she is on her way to death!

– It is true! I have seen it too! It is so sad! And there's nothing we can do about it. You know that, don't you?

– Yes! Unfortunately I do! But how I wish I could free her and bring her back to the arms of her little children...! In their name, she begs for life...!

Panderva is silent, staring into the distance, tears rolling down her face that looks like fine pink porcelain.

Now she watches, almost in shock, the crowd running madly to get to places closer to the imminent execution, granting themselves the "privilege" of collaborating with some sticks of wood for the fire, saying curses and reproaches in chorus with the voices of the executioners.

Admired by Panderva's beauty, elegance and sensitivity, the nobleman approached.

Surprised by the sound of her voice and the affection with which she treats the animal, her perfect features and the tears that reveal her noble feelings, he imagines her in the studio of a skilled painter, portraying her exactly like this: with the little dog on her lap reflecting the compassion and beauty of her soul...

Kindly, he offers her a white handkerchief that has his heraldry embroidered.

Panderva looks him straight in the eye, studies him in silence and ignores his generous offer.

Electrified by her gaze, he is stunned:

– "She is almost ethereal, a goddess fallen from Olympus! Where did this woman come from? Why is she alone? Such elegance, beauty and luminosity!" – He is ecstatic.

He had stepped out of his carriage to observe the events that had impeded him from continuing on his way, and Panderva's presence startled him.

He decided to approach her, he could not resist.

He continues holding the fine embroidered handkerchief, but in a silent gesture, without taking her eyes off him, Panderva turns around and walks away, cuddling the skinny little dog.

Deeply sad, she did not even notice that the nobleman was ecstatic to admire her, until she disappeared completely: "By any chance, while the demons sacrifice the ignorant, the angels descend to earth to cry? This girl is more beautiful than anyone I have seen in the luxurious halls of the court...! If it's not just a mirage, I hope to see her again someday...!"

Finally, he heads towards his illustrious carriage waiting for him in the distance.

Inside the vehicle, a servant dressed in livery greets him warmly:

– Shall we continue, my lord?

– Yes, Matthew! Let's go! I am sorry I cannot do anything to fulfill the wish of the one who was so sad...

– Who, my lord?

– I don't know yet, Matthew, but I will know, believe me, because I will move heaven and earth for it! Her pain touched me so deeply... In that amorous breast I saw a precious sensibility...!

– Did all this happen in a few moments, my lord?

– Well, well, have you forgotten that I have the gift of divination, Matthew? – He says with a frank and sonorous laugh.

– Ah, my lord Theobald! Always joking! I do not even know when you are serious or not!

– Maybe you should not now! – He replies with an enigmatic smile.

The carriage runs wildly towards its destination and Theobald falls into soft reveries, while the vehicle gradually disappears into the streets.

Panderva, who has arrived at her shelter, places the puppy on the ground and sits down beside him to rest.

As she caresses it to calm him down, she remembers Wladimir's words and invitation. You will think about it... Don't be in a hurry!

After all, it will be a very difficult decision! Living with Forbes will be quite an adventure! The two of them argue almost all the time: she orders and Panderva refuses to obey.

In fact, she even takes a certain pleasure in defying her...

A playful smile appears on her face as the puppy lies down next to her and gets comfortable, still feeling full from the food. In this place, Panderva feels at home, free and in control of herself.

Norbert arrives home to find his father immersed in his thoughts.

– Hello, father! The news is bad, isn't it?

– Yes, listen...

Wladimir tells him everything and also includes Panderva's request. No matter how busy or distressed he is, he never ignores anyone's request. Everyone deserves his attention and respect.

Norbert refuses to comment on the day he had; perhaps worse than the others. That would only increase his concern.

His father; however, understands without him saying anything. After a good conversation and dinner, each goes to their rooms to do their duties. There is always plenty to do.

Norbert was very pleased to know that "someone," through Panderva, had alerted his father to the dangers and even had blessed him! Undoubtedly, his father deserved the attention of heaven...

Despite being wary of their own safety, father and son slept peacefully and awoke the next morning for another day of what they hoped would be routine activities.

4.– THE PROVINCIAL COURT

Activities at the provincial court were already underway when Norbert arrived.

Willing to work, as he usually does on a fixed schedule, he faced difficulties with various habitual procedures. There was a patent irritation in everyone and, in the air, something indefinable, more threatening than before...

The work was finally carried out amidst useless and unfounded discussions, which dispersed the thoughts of almost everyone in useless commotion.

The patent insecurity foreshadows the storm brewing over all heads, more for some and less for others.

At the end of the day, Norbert, exhausted, cannot go on.

Overcome by great fatigue, he sits dejected and silent. His large dark robe is spread out on the seat. With his head down, he just wants to get home as soon as possible. His short, noisy breathing and his throbbing forehead reveal his displeasure.

He begins to sweat so he takes off his cloak and pours himself some water to cool off.

The days have been like this; one worse than the other.

How long will they resist the strong pressure exerted by the State and the Church?

Their intention is to put the blame on those who annoy them, and even if they find no legal means for the accusations, they always find a way to invent a well-planned slander.

Trembling, Norbert is certain that his fate, that of his father and many others, must already be decided.

Reflective, he feels someone's gaze and presence. He looks around and sees the familiar and scary figure of Aristophanes.

Standing under one of the wide doorways, his archenemy smiles silently.

He gives him a menacing look, firm and unafraid.

Minutes later, Aristophanes slowly walks backwards, like a hungry beast choosing the best strategy to attack.

– "This bird of ill omen always crosses my way and my father's..."– He concludes.

He can feel his hatred, spite, envy and his bad intentions.

He compares it to a crow swinging and disputing over the carrion scraps.

That evening, Norbert prepares to return home, doubting that his honorable work in the provincial court will last for long...

5.– THEOBALD

Panderva, who is seriously thinking about accepting Wladimir's invitation, has been visiting his house more frequently.

Once there, she observes everyone's routine from a different angle, imagining herself among them.

The little dog is no longer so scrawny due to the generous food rations he receives. Lively, from time to time he enters the house, but ends up being chased away by Forbes, between shouts and complaints.

When this happens, he hides under the stairs, where he feels safer.

This is one more reason for Panderva to fight with Forbes.

Cyrene, poor thing, in the midst of these disputes, feels very worried about what the situation will be like when the girl decides to live here.

Theobald often walks through the same streets, hoping to see the beautiful woman who seems to have captured his heart. Unfortunately, she never crossed his path again... Once, he thought he had seen her, but when he looked for her, he saw no one...

In fact, it was Panderva, who, upon seeing him, sneaked out and fled down roads he didn't know, disappearing from his angle of vision.

She would feel very bad if he found out who she was and how she lived.

Discouraged, Theobald returned to his carriage, ordering the coachman to return home. And he left, immersed in his romantic reverie:

– "What can I do to see that angel again? Was it just a dream? No! I saw her in all her beauty and fascination and, more than that, I spoke to her! We talked...!"

Once home, he resumes his usual activities. He needs to manage the household and the family's goods.

From a very young age, he became accustomed not only to administer, but also to give orders, sometimes with a whip in his hands.

Discouraged and saddened by the failure of his search, which becomes tedious and useless, he goes up to his room.

– Yes, Theobald, you have encountered your past once again...! What does the future hold for you? –

There, bent over papers and documents, he works tirelessly.

His mood, which was not at its best, became even worse because of the intense frustration with which he has come to live.

At night, when he rests, he remembers, detail by detail, everything he experienced that day of joys and surprises.

Between silk sheets, a lot of comfort and economic stability, he does not even imagine that the one he is looking for sleeps in the streets, without any security and with a fragile little dog to keep her company...

From what he had seen, he imagined her protected and well served, in a beautiful mansion or a castle, among silks, lace and jewels, walking proudly and elegantly among her subjects. Or maybe happy with a husband!

At this thought, Theobald jumps out of bed: "I go crazy imagining her married or engaged...! Time may be my greatest enemy and take her away from me! If that hasn't already happened...!"

He cannot leep. His thoughts prevent him from doing so. He gets up and goes out to the balcony full of flowers that give off a fine and delicious perfume.

He leans over and contemplates the beautiful night, as he boringly watches those wandering around in search of something of value, or who knows, conspiring to assault passersby or residences without security guards.

– "Certainly, Theobald! Today you decided to suffer the pains of hell...!"

He gives up staying on the balcony and returns to his room, but does not manage to rest until dawn.

The next morning, he feels unable to fully carry out his tasks.

In another reality and on the same night, Panderva tosses and turns on the cold, rough floor, covered with a soft blanket given to her by Forbes and another equally good one. She dreams until a serene smile appears on her beautiful face.

Before going to sleep, she remembered that elegant and kind gentleman who offered her his handkerchief...

She could not deny it, he exceeded her expectations...! Where had she seen that face, that elegance, that proudness, that affectionate voice? It seemed so familiar to her... How beautiful, elegant and sophisticated!

That day; however, aware of her own reality, she felt the weight of all that she was and how she lived.

She knows that, if she were poorly dressed, he wouldn't even have noticed her presence... That's so obvious...! So why should she remember that event?

Between sleep and vigil, she whispers to herself:

– One day I loved someone like that and that love was my misfortune! But when did this happen? I must get away from him... As I looked at him, my heart accelerated and a longing oppressed my soul...

Weakly, almost asleep, she whispers, still:

– Stay away from me, with all your nobility, unknown sir!

6.– PROVOCATIONS

Wladimir, who has not been at the Provincial Court for a few days, observes that Norbert comes back from there more and more exasperated. How much time will they have? How many days do they have before the big storm breaks out?

He embraces his son and asks him affectionately:

– How are you, son?

Rebellious and with the disturbing image of Aristophanes, he cannot contain himself:

– We are approaching the crater of the volcano roaring beneath our feet!

Wladimir takes a deep breath and comments:

– In spite of everything, my son, we are together and we are aware of this sad reality!

– Yes! I can feel the dissatisfaction and general destabilization settled in the hearts and minds of those who work with us! I feel like facing our enemies with an open heart! My blood is boiling in my veins, father!

– I know you very well and I know how you react! I too endure, like so many others, the persecution of these men maddened by power! Their souls must have forgotten the sovereign law that governs everything, poor unfortunates! If the Creator did not allow it, they would not even breathe! They are dishonored beings who create abysses and walk by themselves!

As your father and friend, Norbert, I must evoke your reason, I ask you to be calm and prudent! Do not give them greater motives than those they conceive in their dark minds! Sooner or later, we know, they will attack! Until then, we must keep our senses alert, watch and pray with great faith, so that God will defend us, give us strength and take our destiny into his providential and loving hands.

At such moral strength and faith, Norbert calms his heart and shakes his father's hand, showing his agreement.

Wladimir, at this point, already has tears in his eyes.

– Believe me, father, this outburst is just a way to ease my soul! If I ever lose control, remind me of my honor and dignity!

Wladimir stands up and hugs him. The words die in his throat. There is nothing more to say, but a lot to feel…and to fear…

Norbert hasn't mentioned that Aristophanes, like a bird of prey, lives to pursue him in the various departments of the Forum, but guesses that he has been doing the same with his father.

It is when he thinks of this cruel man that his soul is most disturbed. He knows; however, that this is exactly where his greatest challenge is.

Embraced, father and son enter the house. They know that their enemies know the cruelest ways to torment those who perform their duties with dedication and honesty, but they trust in God's mercy and there is no greater strength.

7.– DREAM AND REALITY

Despite her own decisions regarding this fortuitous and mysterious encounter, Panderva became more vain.

Theobald's interest in her and his courtesy awakened her feminine vanity.

Gradually, despite having refused some procedures, she becomes better educated, accepts to dress more elegantly, starts to maintain a better hygiene, and tries to establish a more adequate social life.

For Forbes, it's like taking the valuable items stored and preserved in a safe and using them for the benefit of Panderva herself.

Despite her rebelliousness, she is a born lady: elegant, intelligent, cultured and friendly with people.

Cyrene, an attentive observer, remembers her daughter of the same age and immediately understands the reasons for Panderva's vanity. He smiles and inwardly wishes her to be happy.

Now Forbes is able to get along better with Panderva.

Wladimir and Norbert, too busy, do not notice her presence. Panderva enters and leaves by the routes she knows, respecting their privacy and when she thinks it is convenient, she will look for them to find out about her origin.

8.– PACT

Between one providence and another, the powerful in politics and religion gather in a hectic coven to devise definitive plans to get those who bother them out of their way.

Like new Caesars who woke up from their millenary slumber, they decide who should live and who should die – Hail, Caesar! –.

Taking everything and imposing themselves with violence, they dominate with an iron fist. After all, they take it for granted that everything belongs to them and if God permits it, it must be so…! And who could even dare to question them?!

With them, Holy Mother Church will never, never be weakened or deprived of her divine and unique place…!

– God is with us…! – shouts the leader, arrogant and exalted.

– Yes! God will be with us until the end of time…! – The group responds in a tone of sung prayer.

– Even kings bow, without refutation! Let no earthly power dare to challenge us, for we are God's direct representatives!

For those who recklessly challenge us, we will provide them with very effective means of repentance! We know well the proper procedures for repentance and salvation!

The group claps loudly and enthusiastically.

Then, everyone embraces and treats each other with affection.

Once their emotions calm down, they prepare to discuss their common interests.

They exchange information, favors, secrets and make diabolical pacts, focused on dominating minds and hearts, preserving the power they represent, defending what they have and what they desire. There is no ground they cannot tread in order to have absolute control of everything.

The meeting ends with the scheduling of others on predetermined dates.

They celebrate the "sublime expectations" and "clamorous victories" to come, drinking a magnificent wine, accessible only to their kind.

After hours of libation and unethical behavior they take their leave.

Drunk, they get into, or rather, are pushed in their luxurious carriages of "respectable" heraldry by those in charge of serving them.

They will pass quickly through the populace, almost running them over, and if that happens, what can they do?... besides being useless, they are very imprudent!

Upon arriving at their opulent residences, all legally acquired, even though the former residents and owners have been imprisoned, dispossessed or killed, to persuade them to hand them over, the servants, after getting them out of the vehicles, take them to their beds. When they are ready to help them change their clothes, they are subjected to all forms of aggression and reproach.

At that time, as had often happened in the history of civilization, great brave men faithful to the truth were sacrificed and set aside, after suffering all forms of humiliation and pain, like the martyrs of the Roman circuses, and many of them returned to our world, several times to continue, without fear, in the fight of good against evil for the establishment of true progress.

Full of love, they return to confront those who are almost always the same: those fools who wish to destroy and defy all laws, challenging God Himself with their wiles, building a sinister reign of pain and failure on Earth.

9.– MATTHEW AND CYRENE

Today, Matthew is at the service of his boss's heart.

He has known the city very well for a long time, so he has the task of discovering the identity and address of the beautiful young lady who, without knowing it, became the target of Theobald's dreams.

Thus, he has already wandered through streets, hills, alleys and beautiful avenues. In one of these tours, he decided to take advantage of the knowledge of his old friend Cyrene, who has been working for years in the noble house of Mr. Wladimir and Mr. Norbert Vladosk.

The latter, highly respected in Florence, must know many people, even if only by the profession they exercise under the laws of the State.

He knocks on the door and is greeted with a warm welcome:

– Well, well, Matthew! Who's alive always shows up, huh? After all, this city is not so big! Give me a big hug, my dear friend!

Matthew accepts the invitation and embraces him with great happiness:

– Yes, it's true! Here we are! It is great to see you again! I see you are doing great!

– And you look in such good health! You look great! Who would have thought that we have already endured big storms, right?

– But we survived to continue the battle!

– Sit down and tell me, my friend, what's next, surely you must be working this time!

Laughing heartily, Matthew replies:

– Yes! You are very observant!

– As it should be! One eye on life and one eye on the world!

– You are right! What brings me here is not just a longing for old times, but a serious inquiry from my boss. Listen...

He tells of the torments his boss is currently experiencing in search of the beautiful young lady he met on the street.

Cyrene quickly concludes:

– "Panderva...! Who else would act like that? Who could be more beautiful than the one he left well-dressed in the competent care of Forbes? He knew that sooner or later this would happen... Ah...! This is why she is vainer now...! How could he tell Matthew that "that girl" does not belong to his boss's world? If only Theobald knew where and how Panderva lives... However, he would never know, because I will never betray the trust of this dear girl, nor will I be too hasty!

I need to talk to my boss... "– he considers.

Matthew respects his silence and, while he waits, sips a drink and eats tasty cookies. Courtesy of the house. After such an exhausting walk, he is hungry.

Finally, Cyrene speaks up:

– I have thought a lot and I do not know who she is! I will talk to my bosses and if they know anything, I will let you know!

– All right, old friend! Thanks for your attention! See you later and have a nice day!

– You too! It was a pleasure to see you again!

They say goodbye with another hug.

Cyrene resumes his duties.

Humming, Forbes runs into him in the hallway and asks him what Matthew wanted.

– Nothing important, Forbes! He asked me for some information and I gave it to him!

– Ah...! –. She is suspicious of his response. She knows Cyrene enough to know that he is lying... Anyway, she goes about her business and forgets about it.

She orders the clothes that belonged to her mistress, Mrs. Isolde, the dear deceased wife of Wladimir Vladosk. For a long time, the lords of the house have commissioned her to guide them in the best possible way, without refuting about it.

Lately, Panderva is vainer. She likes to look beautiful and well-dressed.

Forbes never got married and never had children. But she learned to love Panderva very much. If she comes to live there, despite their disputes, she will feel less lonely.

On his return, Matthew tells his boss about his useless search.

– Why, Matthew! Was this beautiful woman just passing through Florence?

– Maybe she was, boss, maybe she was!

– That would be catastrophic, but if so, I will extend my search as far as I can! Nothing and no one will stop me from finding her!

– If you wish, I will keep looking for her, my lord!

– Be alert, Matthew, for any sign! Keep your eyes and ears open!

– Yes, my lord! – Matthew bows respectfully and leaves. Then he remembers the thoughtful silence of Cyrene... Perhaps he knows who the mysterious woman is, but what would tie his tongue preventing him from speaking? Probably obedience to his bosses...

He prefers not to say anything about it to Theobald...

When Wladimir arrives home, Cyrene tells him that he needs to talk to him.

– Is the matter urgent, Cyrene?

– No sir! Nothing that requires haste!

– All right, give me a few minutes. Then, I will listen to what you have to say!

– Yes, sir! The problem has to do with our protégée, Panderva.

– Is she well?

– Very well!

Wladimir enters the house in silence.

In the Provincial Court he felt, more than ever, the persecution of his opponents. This time without subtleties.

He can no longer bear to see the anguish of his son.

If they decide to face them, they will be slaughtered with arbitrary measures, and they will face constant brutality of those who seem to enjoy physical and moral pain of unfortunate ones who fall under their cruel tortures and executions...

If they decide to leave, they will be considered cowards and will intimately feel exactly that way.

Those who are as enlisted as they are will, according to their own strength and possibilities, face the same risks.

Like Norbert, he would like to defend himself legally, but he has seen many times where this courage leads: the guilty are acquitted and the innocent are taken to prisons to walk the dark and fatal path of a sinister and undignified death...

He suffers for himself and for Norbert. He is so young... His burning heart seems to be seriously compromised.

You need to think of yourself and of your feelings...

10.– THE MUSE

On his way home, Norbert sees, through the carriage windows, a beautiful woman crossing the street.

Her blonde braids around her ears are long and curly; her face resembles that of an elegantly painted angel; her small feet, wearing colorful shoes and rich handicrafts, run through the streets, careful and light as feathers. In her hands she had little packages, probably some purchases.

Her maid waits for her on the other side of the street and they both get into a luxury vehicle decorated with a coat of arms.

As they pass him, she blushes slightly as she gives him a discreet smile that warms and lights up Norbert's heart.

She is his inspirational muse, his ideal made woman; the reason for his life and his dearest desires.

Ever since he saw her and exchanged glances, his purest and most ardent feelings had turned towards her.

He goes to all the places she frequents to see her, even if only from a distance, because her father, a German nobleman, besides keeping her under strict surveillance, is the friend and companion of his worst enemies.

Odorico Von Braun is jealous of his daughter and plans for her a marriage worthy of her lineage.

When Norbert first saw the beautiful Brunilda and when their eyes met, they vibrated in unison, for her feelings were reciprocal.

– "Our apparently chance meeting must have been the result of a conspiracy of the gods or a beautiful prank by Eros, under the orders of Aphrodite...!" – Norbert thinks, between smiles of delight... In that moment, face to face. as if they were old acquaintances, they exchanged a few words, placing there a lovely mistletoe to unite their souls definitively and irretrievably.

However, the well-mannered maid did not like Brunilda's behavior at all. She approached and suddenly pulled her away from that fascination, dragging her through the streets, turning to see with annoyance that Norbert boldly was following them.

On the other hand, she warned him with resentful eyes of the risk he was running... A few quarters of an hour later, noticing his insistence, she drove her to the carriage waiting nearby and ordered the coachman to take them away as quickly as possible.

From that day on, Norbert lives in suspense: nothing is more important than the blue eyes of that woman of enraptured beauty. When he manages to see her, he is carried away by intense emotions he has never experienced before.

She, in turn, reveals her reciprocated feelings when they meet.

Norbert has already been able to talk to her a few times.

On one occasion, when her delicate hand rested on a sales counter in a store, he caressed her, silently and intentionally transmitting to her the ardor of his passion.

That day, after sending her maid away to buy something, Brunilda arranged a small recess so that they could introduce themselves.

The coachman, Percival, already knows the boy and every time he sees him, he gives him a kind and sympathetic look.

Besides feeling sorry for the domestic prison in which the beloved young woman lives, Norbert once defended him.

Grateful for that, he admires the boy who, when he defends his ideals, in an atmosphere of silence, respect and admiration, silences his opponents.

For that, Percival is already a potential friend that Norbert can count on, which is evident in the smile of encouragement he gives him. He thinks Brunilda is lucky to have attracted the interest of a man like Norbert Vladosk: upright, handsome, elegant and wealthy.

Of course, he does not wear heraldry, like his family, but he can always buy it if he wants to. The means for that are not lacking.

Norbert has a distressed soul, analyzing unfavorable circumstances. At any moment, life can definitely split them apart. How to survive without her?

Brunilda is his north, his light, his hope for happiness! To his surprise, he found himself loving her desperately. He usually rejects any feeling that could stop him. The loss of his emotional freedom was never in his plans, but today he lives amidst the torments of uncertainty in this surprising and insurmountable feeling.

He lives at the same time a challenge of life and death, facing what lurks in the sinister shadows of the thoughts and intentions of his declared enemies.

Perhaps life will demand of him and his father a strategic escape from Florence. If that happens, what will he do with this love? Leave Brunilda behind? Never...!

She is fully aware that her father, the baron, will soon marry her off to someone of his choice, especially when he finds out that she is interested in someone who does not live up to his expectations.

Under these circumstances, Brunilda, like so many others, is a bargaining chip on the stock market for his ambitions.

Thinking about it, Norbert almost loses control.

He must talk it over with his father, after all, today everything will depend on that love. He cannot even imagine himself away from Florence or away from her.

An anticipated feeling of loss grips him and makes him suffer. Lately, he has been remembering the almost fatal situation he experienced in childhood with his father. The images of that day never left his memory and what challenges him today may be as dangerous as... Will they make an honorable and favorable exit?

"Poor dear father, he too receives threats and disrespect and is counting on my participation to satisfactorily resolve our near future... How to reconcile all these issues and give them the right direction?"

At that moment, he walks nervously in the spacious and beautiful room of his house.

He stops to reflect and resumes his restless pacing several times, but sees no solution for the moment.

When his father arrives, he decides to approach him:

– My son, you look very worried. Can I help you? Besides our own situation, is there anything else bothering you?

Sitting down, he finally confesses:

– Yes, I have other worries, my father, and these weigh as much as the others! Father you have been my witness for some time now, I have struggled between reason and heart and finally find myself in love, or, rather, truly in love with a woman who sums up everything a man could wish for. But...

Norbert pauses, while Wladimir reveals a growing anxiety.

– There is always a but, isn't it? Well, this woman who today completely dominates my senses, my heart and my soul, is the only daughter of Odorico Von Braun. As you can see, today I struggle between the fortunes of heaven and the torments of hell; between hopes of happiness and fear of losing her...

Wladimir sighs and puts his hand to his chest. He already predicted something similar. If it had been an easy challenge to face, his son would have already told him.

– I am sorry to hear that, my son! We already have so many problems and this one is not far behind...! We know the huge obstacles women face when they love. Between their love and their will, there is almost always the authority of the father and the family as a whole.

We are fully aware that the laws in force explicitly protect the father's power. We fight against these laws every day and this stone wall prevents us from reaching justice! We work uselessly in the face of these disputes and almost always fail to achieve the desirable solutions!

Wladimir, more and more upset, continues:

– We have seen innumerable tragedies because of these disputes that the power of the family disposes and enshrines upon its descendants.

It seems that our progress is in a cart and that only one of the wheels keeps it on the road, that of hope, which is firm and still exists thanks to the affection and dedication of those who, looking beyond, know that no one has the power to prevent the choices of the heart...!

How long, oh Lord of the Universe, how long will we crawl like worms on the ground, filthy with the fetid mud of our moral imperfections...?!

Norbert is deeply moved by such positive and lucid speech.

– "This is my father...!" – He thinks proudly and feeling respect.

With eyes full of emotion, he listens to him with adoration, almost forgetting his own existential conflicts.

Wladimir stops, calms down, undoes his defensive posture and sits down in front of his son:

– Tell me everything, I beg you! Together we will be able to better assess the situation that really seems as serious as those we have already faced; You said it and I confirm it!

Norbert opens his heart and narrates everything from the beginning, without forgetting to mention that, for the good fortune of his soul, his love is fully reciprocated.

– What should I do, father? My God, is there a way out of this impasse safely and with her by my side?

– Who knows, Norbert, a good circumstance will happen in due time.

– Wouldn't it be too much to hope, my father?

– We have been through difficult situations before. The men with whom we interact and who claim to be the sole and direct representatives of the Creator ignore His mercy and His justice...! Blinded, they spread their evils and do not even fear the "day of reckoning." However, beloved son, we know of divinity and His presence in our lives. We cannot forget the unexpected and blessed warning we received through the "oracle" we know so well! I believe that the girl who has captured your heart is part of your destiny and has arrived at the right time! We can conclude that she too awaits your decisions!

Norbert agrees, breathing heavily:

– We Will have to know what to do, when and how! I hope so... Shall we dine? Hunger, despite our misfortunes, comes at the right time!

Together, they enter the large dining room, where the servants are already eager to serve them.

They sit down and eat with pleasure. This is always a time of joy and comfort for both of them.

When they finish, they both head to their respective rooms. In the evening, Norbert admires the stars and compares them to the luminous gaze of his beloved.

There, sighing, like any mortal in love, he spends hours, until fatigue takes over his senses and he goes to sleep, dreaming of Brunilda, first awake and then asleep.

In his dreams, he and the woman of his desire run embraced through flowery fields, exchange caresses, laugh and sing. All around them, the lush beauty of the landscape...

11.– PROVIDENTIAL ZEAL

Dissatisfied with the disillusionments he has been suffering, in terms of looking for the woman he has never seen again and whom he desires so much, Theobald orders Matthew to go out again to look for her.

After his butler leaves, he spends the day restless:

– "Maybe this time he will find something useful? Matthew has a talent for finding lost things, distant people, and a certain facility for solving a variety of problems. He seems to have been born for it."

Obeying, Matthew leaves, this time choosing other paths and other places.

After hours of searching, tired and almost dejected, he decides to talk to his friend Cyrene.

Arriving there, after greeting Cyrene, the latter informs him that Mr. Wladimir wishes to speak to his boss.

With hope, Matthew asks:

– Tell me Cyrene, do you know the girl in question?

– I do not know her, my friend. Without commenting on the fact, he ordered me to tell you this, in case you came back here.

– My boss will certainly come to see you!

– Wait, my friend! I do not think they are meeting here!

– In that case, I will wait! Will you let me know?

Cyrene nods in confirmation and invites him to a meal, but this time Matthew declines the invitation, explaining that his boss might be angry at his delay.

— It is better not to take any risks, my friend!

Then he says goodbye with a warm embrace.

Cyrene informs Wladimir of Matthew's return and he concludes very worriedly:

– "The gentleman is impatiently looking for Panderva... It is understandable... She possesses a remarkable beauty. But he certainly ignores her itinerant life. If he knew, he wouldn't be that interested; it's as clear as a sunny day. Theobald is a seductive man and fond of easy conquests. There is much talk of his love scandals. Let's hope Panderva does not get fooled or dragged into a life worse than the one she already faces... "

Thinking of his son, he concludes:

– "Norbert, in turn, a prisoner of love, will face almost insurmountable barriers, since his beloved belongs to a family viscerally tied to the interests of our archenemies. This girl will never be his wife, unless unexpected and providential events take place that frustrate the expectations of those who decide for her... Poor son, wanted by so many women, he fell into the trap of fate! I wonder how much he must be suffering? ... How can I help him? More than ever, we must be alert and prepared for any eventuality!"

Wladimir takes care of business intensively. Even if he leaves Florence - this possibility grips his heart painfully - he will continue to do so legally and elsewhere.

In the Provincial Court, he has debated extensively about laws that are not enforced and justice that is not exercised as it should.

Deeply immersed in his afflictions and in his work, he did not notice that once again Norbert had been watching him for some time, hesitant to talk to him or not, so as not to interrupt him.

Intuitively, he looks around and observes him there:

– Come in, my son! Do you want to talk to me?

– Yes, if you can, of course!

– If we do not talk here, where and when will we do it, son?

Norbert sits down in front of him:

– Do you already know what to do about the unpleasant situation we are living in?

– Our only alternative would be to agree with the ideas and purposes of our opponents.

– The two of us would never do that...!

– Certainly not! I think of those who stand on their side, often out of fear, to save what they believe belongs to them, starting with their own lives.

– They do not even think of the price they will have to pay! Fools! While they think they live, they commit moral suicide!

– As for your love for Brunilda, my son, do you know what to do?

Wladimir fears what his son is about to say.

– I shall cautiously await some sign from Above, as we have already discussed, but I shall be on the lookout for any more propitious occasion to act quickly. Father, Imagine, I, being an undisputed admirer of bards and muses, of all the high forms of art and culture, have met a woman who amazes me and fulfills all my yearnings as a man and as aesthete!

Smiling proudly, Wladimir says:

– Your luminous soul possesses great knowledge, my son.

Moved, Norbert declares:

– My soul surrendered to this love!

– Are you happy?

– Completely happy!

– Whatever happens, this great love will compensate for the sorrows and difficulties along the way. So was life for me with your dear and beloved mother...

Longing and reverent, Wladimir pauses a little, as if he were going back in space and time...

After a few moments, he concludes:

– Even if fate twists our paths, we will follow the inspiration of our soul and our own reason, trusting above all in the Creator, who is just, but also merciful.

– This is how we have always lived!

– Good omens for your love, Norbert! I hope to soon meet this woman who fascinated the heart of my only son!

– I thank you! As for introducing her... If it were up to me, she would already be here in our house.

– Let us wait, then...

They continued to talk about many other things that concerned them.

✳ ✳ ✳

Despite the tragedies of that time full of darkness, men of virtue and faithful to God challenged the malice and arbitrariness of the tyrants.

They disappeared or were sacrificed in the name of their "blasphemies and dangerous ideas – since the time of Socrates we know the tragic and luminous destinies of these stars of God –."

Despite their sufferings and often premature deaths, they left us the facet of progress they carried in their hands like rays of light, through the courage that distinguished them, often culminating in painful testimonies.

Humanity has always trusted them in the most diverse sectors of life, in different continents, because they were sent by the governor of this planet, who does not forget, nor moves by chance.

✲ ✲ ✲

Panderva arrives and is told that Wladimir needs to talk to her.

Hopeful, she waits anxiously for his arrival. Perhaps his friend already knows something about her origins.

She accepts the warm welcome, as always, and goes out a couple of times to feed his little dog, who already feels he owns the space under the stairs of the rich residence.

The hours seem to drag on forever, filling her heart with hope.

Cyrene and Forbes, who attend to the young woman, presume that the subject in question is not the one she imagines; however, they cannot and should not interfere.

Clean, as she lives at present, well dressed and very pretty, she is awaiting the interview.

She has left the pilgrimages behind. Little by little, she changes her old habits and calms down.

Dividing her time between the street, her old acquaintances and life there, she is less angry with poor Forbes, who, tired and full of rheumatic pains, does not always manage to have the tolerance she should.

Late in the afternoon, Wladimir arrives, eats and goes to his office, where he requests Panderva's presence. When he sees her arrive, he invites her to sit down, which she does delicately and anxiously.

– Does the good man wish to speak with me? – she asks timidly and somewhat fearful.

– Yes!

Silently, she waits for Wladimir to speak.

– Panderva, I wanted to talk to you because I was informed that someone is looking for you.

– That's not possible! I don't mess with anyone! You know that!

– Yes, I know, relax! Someone met you by chance in the street, and never saw you again. Since then, very interested, he has been looking for you. His butler, Matthew, is a friend of Cyrene and came here to ask for information.

Panderva blushes a lot and lowers her gaze. Her heart beats madly.

Wladimir asks:

– Do you remember anyone?

– Yes! One day, when I came across a tenebrous procession, led by religious men who in a ritual would consummate the tragedy of a poor woman, surely accused of something she wasn't even sure of... Terrified and deeply grieved, I cried a lot and ended up losing my strength. A nobleman approached me and spoke to me quickly, besides offering me his handkerchief to wipe my tears...

– And what else? – Wladimir feels uneasy and very worried. He knows Panderva well and noticed her remarkable embarrassment.

Lifting her face, she replies:

– Nothing else! I listened to his opinion about what happened, but I refused his kindness and left.

Increasingly flushed and gloomy, she commented:

– I know that if he had known whom he was talking to with such kindness, this would never have happened, because this conceited nobleman would have stayed away from me, like all the others!

– I am glad to see that, in spite of everything, you have wise and prudent thoughts. Well, this nobleman wants to know if we know you!

Almost in shock, Panderva asks quietly:

– And what did you tell him?

– Nothing, dear friend! Calm down! Well instructed by me, Cyrene and Forbes said nothing. First of all, I want to know what you think!

Panderva says:

– Thank you...

– Well, Panderva, this man is interested in you, what do you want to do?

She answers with another question:

– Why did your butler come looking for me right here?

– Matthew is looking for you all over town! He was here to find out if his friend Cyrene knew anything. That's all.

– Ah...! What a relief!

– I plan to talk to him, but don't worry! I just want to know what his true intentions are and nothing else! He will never know that we know.

– Thank you in the name of God!

– Despite our secrecy, Panderva, sooner or later he will find you, and when that happens, what will you do? Moreover, what do you really think and feel for him?

Completely disconcerted, Panderva feels the urge to escape… In front of this good friend, she feels uncovered. Given his precise and competent analysis of a wise and good man… Increasingly intimidated, she responds carefully:

– I think this is just another challenge in my life, and one of the worst!

– Why?

– Because people like that gentleman do not mix! He must look down on everyone! Even if I live clean and well-dressed, I will always be someone with nothing, with an unknown origin, no whereabouts, no ties, no family, and… no noble lineage!

She is on the verge of tears.

Wladimir feels great sorrow and concludes with lament:

– "She shows no disinterest… She only analyzes the impossibility… Perhaps she is more involved than she thinks…"

Determined to be honest, knowing that he could never hide information from Panderva, he decided to advise her:

– Dear daughter, reflect on what you really feel before you listen to what I have to tell you.

Determined, she raises her head haughtily and asks:

– You can speak freely! Life has taught me to bear the full weight of adversity and face the truth! Speak and be very sincere, I beg you!

Despite being brave, Panderva would like not to be there, not to hear anything more… She knows that her crazy illusions will lose color and hope, as soon as her dear friend unravels the rosary of information on which sweats the soul of a woman that loves passionately still and always...!

Guessing his dear friend's thoughts and lamenting her future suffering, Wladimir knows he cannot let her go without warning her of the possible battle she will face, from which she, only she, will be injured...

So he begins to tell her everything he knows. He hides nothing. She deserves honesty and clarity, as does everyone around her. Moreover, she is completely defenseless, compared to this experienced and seductive man, in a world that belongs almost exclusively to her and against which she has no defenses...

When he finished speaking, Panderva is sad, although she tries to hide her disappointment.

Overcoming the urge to cry, she declares:

– This is how I judged him that day... He carries within him the living image of his own actions. It all sounds false and dangerous...

– How did you manage to analyze him so well?

– I didn't do it only on that occasion!

– So you already knew each other?

– Yes and no!

– Can you explain it better?

– I will try! Seeing him looking at me the way he did, I "felt" I had the knowledge, and I know more about him than he does!

– With your gifts?

– I think so!

– Anyway, Panderva, how do you feel about him?

– I am attracted to him, but at the same time something in me strongly rejects him, as if he represented some sort of danger. When my eyes were fixed on his, something took me to a time that I cannot recall, but which must have generated in my soul those feelings of attraction and repulsion. What amazed me most was to see myself in the depths of his eyes and I assure you, what I saw was neither praiseworthy nor beautiful to behold...! Unfortunately, he is still the same! Woe betide him, woe betide us...!

Although I chose redemptive paths, he preferred the same paths again to return to power and wealth! We must stay away, unless God wants to test us...!

Panderva is speaking almost to herself. Her voice is getting fainter and fainter... The pain she feels is legitimate and rises from her good soul to her overexcited heart and nerves, immersed in sensations that transcend the present reality.

– Panderva, you surprise me, always! I admire that refined perception of yours! Anyway, what do you decide?

She replies honestly:

– Do what you think is necessary, I know you will always do what is best! You are good, besides being very wise!

– I thank you! I will do my best to protect you!

The girl stands up, gives a small nod of respectful farewell and runs through the door.

She passes Cyrene, who can barely speak to her, and runs wildly towards her "place", along with those who live like her, without destiny, without origin, without hope...

Wladimir is speechless. Sadly, he understood that she struggles with an old love, which with the passage of time has been restored in her new existence for future experiences.

– "Your future, dear child, is a great incognita! May God protect you, because I myself cannot imagine how this will develop from now on!" – He concludes.

Absorbed, he sees Cyrene appear at the door, wordlessly asking the reason for the girl's hasty departure.

– Don't worry, Cyrene! She needs time to think. When she's better, she will be back, don't worry! She has a safe place here! Wait a minute, I will write a note that you must take with you as soon as possible!

Wladimir writes making an appointment at the provincial court with Theobald.

– Take this to Matthew and as for Panderva, be very discreet! Let us not be instruments of torture for her. After all, Panderva has already suffered enough!

Cyrene agrees and leaves with the missive.

When he sees Forbes, he tells her the boss's recommendation. Wladimir continues to reflect on Theobald:

– "Just as the wolf follows the trail of his prey, so this man will stubbornly pursue her wherever she is, and Panderva, unloved and bound to him from before, will be easy prey..."

Seeing Panderva, the dog runs in pursuit.

Arriving at her favorite place, Panderva settles in as best she can and hugs the little animal, caressing it.

When Norbert learns what happened, he insists on the urgency of investigating Panderva's origins, since in this or any other circumstance, she will always be at a great disadvantage.

As night falls, everyone seeks rest, including the girl who can do everything possible. Cozy with her dear "friend", in a few minutes she falls asleep and dreams that she is in her castle and their reigns powerful and absolute...

– Oh, dear spirit! While this will serve you as a comfort and support for current tests, I praise the Creator; however, that it does not only serve to deceive your soul thirsty for transformation...!

12.– OBSESSION...

The obstacles Wladimir and his son are facing increase, becoming unbearable.

Those who seek the doom of both exert pressure, spreading it through all the departments of the provincial court, in a dismal web.

The once solid ground is now quicksand.

These challenges foretell the worst! There is no doubt of a sad epilogue.

It is urgent to decide what must be done promptly, before it is too late...!

The presence of Aristophanes is constant. Before, from time to time he would appear imposing and evaluating everything, with his prey-like gaze along with the power he represents.

He, a frightening figure, authorized by the Church and the State, cunning and cruel, stubbornly pursues those who work there, but do not agree to what is done and, instead, react against the order and the laws that have their "variants" to suit different interests and maintain order.

Personally, Wladimir and Norbert are the ones who bother him the most; however, his rage for pursuing them today has another aggravating factor: friend and guest in the baron's house, Aristophanes carries in his dark heart another motive, very particular, because when he met Brunilda, owner of an exuberant Nordic beauty, besides being – oh, what a surprise! – the only heiress of Baron Odorico Von Braun, he experienced an unbridled desire to conquer her.

To have it and all that would come with it, he will use all the resources he has, in addition to the resources he knows like no one else.

It is no coincidence that, at his proximity, many tremble with fear.

In any case, he will drive away the other suitors, especially the son of Wladimir Vladosk, whom he cannot stand.

He angrily concludes that Norbert and his father almost always stand in his way...! It is impossible to ignore that some strange spell binds them together, as if they were fatally bound. However, he is not afraid of Norbert's rivalry. He is confident in his own power and in the privileges he enjoys. He lives attentive to everything that may attempt against his love interests, and at this level, Norbert is his first target.

He sits comfortably and thinks:

– "It has already taken too long to accomplish our *desiderátum*! How hard it is for me to control myself...! We have already woven a proper net and these two fish, not as important as they think they are, will finally travel paths they cannot even imagine...! Face to face with them, one at a time, of course, I will be pleased to hear them beg for mercy, without ever granting it! Ah...! The plans I have for them...! Not even the lord of hell can imagine...! I will fulfill an ancient wish and I will do it whatever it takes...!"

In these thoughts, he does not even remember the One he claims to represent and who reads in the heart as in an open book.

Today, more furious than before, because of the urgency to carry out actions that have already been delayed, he was informed of the visit of an administrator with the two highest powers in his greedy hands: the civil and the religious; and the urgency to prepare his reception with great luxury, reverence and zeal.

This undisputed authority will eventually arrive modifying the usual context of the various levels of interests, whatever they may be.

The mere mention of his name causes disturbance and silence, obstructing anyone's intentions and objectives.

Not even Aristophanes will be able to ignore the orders received directly from the "major command", who, like this unwelcome visitor, has the cards in his hand and dominates, always and, in any way, this game, wherever he is settled.

In this situation, such well-elaborated plans will have to wait for a more appropriate occasion.

Nobody knows what the next few days will be like.

The town simply has to welcome him with a unique nobility and be at his disposal, without demands, without reservations and with service. One false step and...

His hierarchical position and the mystery that surrounds him implies a close connection with the highest powers.

Just as surprises are part of anyone's life, this one will change a lot in Florence.

For this reason, everyone cleverly backs off.

The positive side is that those who are dealing with difficulties created by the political and religious powers, in their worst position, will have more time to act and organize their own defenses. This is also true for Wladimir and his son.

In the luxurious and poorly illuminated environment in which he finds himself, Aristophanes continues to be immersed in his gloomy melancholy. He stands up uneasily and crosses the great hall, thinking, thinking, pausing occasionally to whisper something that only he can understand, and begins to walk again.

He picks up the sword hanging from his waist and clenches it convulsively:

– "Ah, if those in my sights knew, they would not even sleep... Diogenes has already been exemplarily punished, paying me with interest what he owes me! He will never again stand in my way!"

Mixing thoughts and intentions, he ponders his greatest interest:

– "I will win the baron's trust and hold that beautiful woman's hand...! Never before have my eyes rested on such beauty! Stay away from idiot rivals, for I am on the list! For having led this world with so much effort, we, the most direct representatives of the divinity, can and deserve everything, because this commitment to preserve, maintain and enrich Holy Mother Church consumes us...! It is right that we should be the first to be endowed with the graces of earth and heaven!

Woe to those who defy us, for they will enlighten the world in the consummation of their flesh, in the sacred rituals for the purification of their souls!

It is necessary to bring order since bold and reckless personalities appear from all sides, even from the bosom of our most sacred institutions...!"

Immersed in his sinister thoughts, sometimes he hides his features, sometimes he smiles with satisfaction or even bursts into laughter that would make anyone flee from his path.

Afternoon arrives and little by little the bright sun sets. Aristophanes admires himself and his ostentation.

His clothes fit him very well, with an enviable luxury; his jewels that shine in the light that still penetrates through the stained glass windows are true works of art; his bearing is haughty; his body well proportioned. Accustomed to sports and physical fights, he also recognizes that his physiognomic features are very attractive.

– "Women say so! Everywhere I go, I see their greedy looks and hear their sighs, the only thing that would be worth eternal penances for them...!"

– This man will do anything to maintain his position and continue to enjoy the advantages he has already achieved –.

For brief moments, Aristophanes becomes agitated, somewhat uneasy. Life itself and the heaven he claims to represent will sooner or later hold him accountable...!

And what will the hell he threatens so many with be like? When his time comes, will the gates open for him?

How could he know?!

He has already lost himself in so many so-called sacraments!

Dogmas defy everyone and his vain representation of the Holy Office, leaves countless victims...

When will it be his turn to also face the "final judgment"?

He is not and has never been a fool. He knows that he benefits and is an accomplice of an artificial, arbitrary and cruel reign. What he ignores, he can guess.

He has sedimented his own existence in lies, betrayal and crime. He was accustomed to this for many years. Those who created him gave him twisted codes in which he structured his life.

He hates and viscerally envies Wladimir and his son, because they, like others, represent what he himself could have been and never was.

Unusual thoughts; however, not infrequently reach him as they do now:

And when all is over, Aristophanes, who will inherit what you created by selling your own soul? Everything will be left to the mercy of others, or what you possess will be taken away from you in life, in a plot of fate, the kind that surprises so many every day... The system itself gives you a blow, without explanations or defenses...! How can you forget that no one has ever taken with them what they thought they had? And your goods, Aristophanes, where do they come from? He shakes his head and looks around, but the voice that seems to speak within him, telling him things he cannot bear to hear, rises and now speaks with emphasis, echoing throughout the atmosphere:

– When your day comes, Aristophanes, you will receive your rewards, for we will be here, waiting to reward you with due honors!

Annoyed, he curses:

– Damn! Who's there? – He scans, eyes blazing, every nook and cranny, furious and extremely agitated.

– Who dares to speak to me like this? And what shadows are these?! Get out! Get out of here! Get out...! –. Breathless, he tries to expel something from the surroundings that only he can see...

At that moment, the bells ring sadly, and he is stunned...

Where did that voice come from... Who had the audacity...? He goes into the long, dark hallway.

There, a few minutes later, a group of novices appears, singing.

Blocking their way, in a posture of attack and defense, he asks with a thunderous and imposing voice:

– Who spoke loudly here by the door?

They look at each other, silently wondering what the question is about.

– Sir, we have just arrived and are on our way to the Blessed Sacrament chapel!

Speechless, Aristophanes finds no plausible explanation. In a silent bow, the group leaves, not understanding the attitude of the superior.

Aristophanes returns to the same place as before. He cannot lose patience.

His soul is in chaos, his thoughts are at odds...

13.– THE INTERVIEW

Very anxious, Theobald appears at the Provincial Court.

Wladimir beckons him to come closer.

Analyzing the surrounding, he sits down and says:

– All right, here I am!

– Thank you for your punctuality! Allow me a few more minutes!

– I didn't come to watch you work!

Ignoring his impatience, Wladimir shouts:

– Desiderius!

An attractive, pleasant-featured employee enters and receives from Wladimir a package of papers and documents officially signed and stamped.

With a small bow, Desiderius leaves. At a signal from Wladimir, he closes the door.

– Alright, Mr. Theobald! Do you have any idea why I called you here?

– Yes! I hope you have information about the person I am looking for!

– In fact, I booked this interview out of curiosity.

– What?!

– I will explain. When I was informed that your butler was in my house looking for someone you were interested in, I wanted to know the reasons.

Wladimir wants to find out to what extent he knows or does not know about Panderva.

Astonished, Theobald remains silent, considering Wladimir's great audacity in calling him out of the blue.

With a patent fury, he turns purple by rage.

With a faint smile that exasperates him, Wladimir confirms his violent character.

Suddenly standing up, he asks:

– Did you just call me for that?!

– Why? Don't you think my curiosity is fair?

Theobald does not know whether to stay and listen to him or leave.

– It would be a good idea for you to answer my question! And if you calm down and do not forget that we are gentlemen who value courtesy, we can talk. After all, I have an activity that allows me to get to know a lot of people!

Theobald sits down again and, very annoyed, explains:

– Matthew went there, as he went to many other places, in search of information!

– I see... However, dear Count, in my house, it is the women who represent the service corps, in addition to the male servants. Do you know the name of the person in question?

– Unfortunately not! Hence the difficulties.

– Can you at least describe her?

– I will try...

He narrates the casual encounter, while praising the beauty and dominant presence of the woman who seems very interested.

Wladimir concludes, from what he has heard, that he is talking about Panderva.

– Well... Without a more specific point of reference, I can't know who she is. So, you are just left to rely on luck!

– This conversation is getting too vague!

Feigning an exemption of spirit, Wladimir inquires further:

– If you find her, what do you want with her? your interest is remarkable!

Deeply displeased, Theobald asks:

– Who gave you the right to ask me for that? What is your interest?

– One that prescribes the education and nobility proper to every woman, Mr. Theobald!

Clapping his hands and bowing, with the gestures of chivalrous nobility, Theobald jokes:

– Bravo, Bravo! You really make beautiful speeches! However, I hope I never need your action in my defense; your defense is rather doubtful, because it is full of ridiculous and childish moralism...!

– I am not talking about moralism, dear sir, but about morals! Perhaps, in spite of your power, you do not know the distance between these two classifications! And as for the ridiculous, we can see it in abundance in the arrogance of people who, like you, consider themselves above everything and everyone, and surrender to all rights without problems of conscience!

– Hum... I may conclude that you know the lady in question! If not, why the passionate defense?

Wladimir knows that he is dealing with a very cunning fox.

– From your dedicated search, I come to the conclusion that the woman in question must be of great interest to you.

– Maybe! So? – Theobald challenges him, somewhat mockingly.

– If so... although I do not know who you are looking for, I come to the conclusion that she needs defense, especially from God!

– Explain yourself better! – Says Theobald, who stands up and almost throws himself on Wladimir, who remains calm.

– I will do it and gladly! You do not expect respect and discretion to be exercised at every corner in Florence, do you? The acts of anyone are proclaimed to the four winds: by word of mouth, in salons, in garrets, in markets, in kitchens, in taverns and in brothels, and you Mr. Count Theobald of Vila D'Oro wouldn't get away with it! I know who I am talking to, so I will save myself explanations to justify the pity I feel for anyone who comes to interest you!

Snorting like a wild bull, Theobald replies aggressively:

– Now! After all, was I invited to be insulted? Pay attention to my position and do not waste my time with your cheap philosophies! I, unlike you, received from life the privilege of being a nobleman by birth. That's why I do not need you or anyone else! Damn it! What a waste of time! I should never have come here...!

Saying that, Theobald turns his back and heads for the exit.

However, raising his voice, Wladimir advises:

– Do not bet on that! Men like you are the ones who need the law the most!

Turning around, furious, he challenges:

– Are you forgetting that we can use it at our whim or even ignore it?

– Unhappily no! I know "these practices" very well! Finally, everyone chooses their own path and also builds their own future, fragile as a house of cards!

– You certainly do not speak of me, but of you and those of the same level who live downstairs and are trampled underfoot!

– No, Count, I speak of facts and laws of men like the Lord. And here, right now, I can tell you, in case you ignore it, that your statements are dangerously against you!

– Now you use sincerity! You brought me here to hurt me, wasn't that it? May I at least know the reasons for these unreasonable accusations?

– What accusations? You are not in Court! We're just talking and exchanging ideas, have you forgotten? Why on earth would I hurt you? I barely know you and what I know is widely known by everyone! Cheating is not part of my *modus operandi*! My first intention was to find out the reasons why you sent your butler to my house, as I told you! This is all because of your insane stance, disrespect and aggression! Let me also tell you that titles of nobility like yours, inherited at birth or acquired by the power of gold, do not always go hand in hand with those that really distinguish the good citizen from the bad citizen, and almost all have sad stories of life and death!

Coats of arms and heraldry are no one's inalienable rights, as they pass to various people at the mercy of chance and at different times.

Looking at him steady and seemingly calm, Wladimir suggests that the disastrous interview is over.

Silent with hatred, Theobald stares at his opponent and thinks that he would never want to face him in a court of justice:

– "This good man, an exemplary citizen, does justice to his good fame in Florence! He knows who he is and how much he is worth...!"

When he comes to his own conclusions, Wladimir waits in silence for him to leave.

If he were Panderva's father – and he feels that way, in his heart... – this swindler would never approach her. However, only time will tell, given the decisions she will make herself, as the free and intelligent person she is.

Thinking about how much there is left to do, he asks:

– Anything else, Mr. Theobald?

Furious, Theobald heads for the exit. Before he gets there, however, he turns around, rehearses a pronouncement that lingers in the air, and gives up.

Wladimir is unbeatable, there is no point in talking to him or even answering him... He hates this...! Stomping his feet, he walks away, while his soul is restless, then proud and petty, he plans a revenge. No one who dares to offend his pride goes unpunished!

Wladimir sorts some papers, places them in drawers, locks them, picks up his cloak and hat and proceeds to leaves.

With a heavy heart, on his way home, he sadly concludes that Panderva runs a great risk if she is the one Theobald is looking for.

Looking out of the vehicle, he sees a curious and colorful group of acrobats.

Noisy and joyful, they perform their show, dancing to the sound of flutes, maracas, tambourines, bells and fifes, in the midst of wild jumps and gestures of reverence to the public in that beautiful square in Florence.

They throw flyers with funny drawings and information about the group and spread a colorful and perfumed powder on the passersby, performing incredible pirouettes to entertain young and old...

After pleasant and amusing adventures, they head for other places. But before leaving, they ask for water, money and treats.

When they receive them, they thank them with exaggerated bows that only they know how to do.

Smiling and sensing the good intentions of those who, while struggling for survival, show their talents and rejoice other people's hearts, Wladimir orders his coachman to reward them. Empowered by their dreams and reverent to the various art forms, they face all of life's difficulties without losing enthusiasm.

Attentive, some noticed his gentle action. They approach the coachman's window and do their best in amusing him, making him laugh with great pleasure.

Grateful to them all, Wladimir greets them and continues on his way. He admires these people, with great emotion...

In the depths of his heart he does not disdain the desire to live the same experience, in an itinerant life, without many ties, and despite the suffering that affects any mortal, to maintain, in spite of everything, a persistent commitment to happiness...!

– "When I was a humble manual laborer and physical pain overwhelmed me, making me bear the weight of "my cross", I was not unhappy; I carried the longings for the future by the achievements made, by the mercy of God, in my constant effort...

But to everything there is a season, and a time for every purpose under heaven, as the psalm says...!"[4]

As the vehicle swings, he thinks that soon he will be home; his refuge, his sacred space:

---

[4] Ecclesiastes 3:1.

– "Everyone should have "their shelter", everyone! One day, one day! The future will account for and make many changes and impose legitimate progress, in the absence of those who believe that they dominate everything!

For that, time exists, constant and uncontrollable, perennial and master of itself. What a kindness of the divine power to grant us so many opportunities here or in other celestial homes...!

I belonged to the kingdoms of Nature in their different levels of creation, thousands of times... Today I belong to the order of humans, responsible for themselves and for the destiny of the world...!

Thank you, Creator! Divine spark within us...!"

14.– MR. ANASTACIO

Upon his arrival, the usual formalities take place, in addition to the exaggerations of those who try to flatter him from the first moment.

Arrogant and wearing luxurious clothes that reveal his hierarchy and power, Mr. Anastacio observes everything like a harpy.

Accompanied by a large number of prelates, soldiers and servants, he enters the city like a Caesar.

Any action or attitude, even imperceptible as it may seem, does not go unnoticed.

The people, crowded and noisy, are amused, not only by the color and luxury, but also by the servility of those who usually suffocate and despise them. There they bend their necks, in an improvised and hilarious pantomime.

Tired and grumpy, the character in question despises the compliments given to him, but would surely punish them if they did not do so.

Thus, his ornamented and colorful figure imposes itself on everyone, civil and religious. At times like these, those who usually dominate bow to a greater will and submit like little lambs – oh, human hypocrisy! –.

A banquet was organized with everything necessary to welcome him and until nightfall, visitors, guests and representatives of the powers of the city gather, despite having radically opposing ideas.

Thus, in spite of any other will, there is a truce in the different interests.

The civil and religious authorities were accompanied by their relatives, vainly displaying their most pompous possessions.

As expected, the baron and his daughter are in the first place.

Speeches and eulogies are carried out, which wear out and fatigue even those to whom the honors are addressed.

praises and making oneself visible is a necessity, after all, opportunities like these cannot be overlooked! Footmen and servants, numerous, barely enough to serve so many people.

The public coffers, of course, covered most of the expenses, in addition to the "generous donations" of the Church and of some citizens of Florence, interested in being noticed.

Wladimir and Norbert are there, embarrassed and deeply upset. Their highly representative positions make it impossible for them to evade social demand, especially now, when their absences can easily be labeled as offenses.

Seeing them, the baron cannot hide his displeasure. He quickly takes steps to restrict his daughter's freedom, keeping her under strict surveillance.

Together and on the fringes of the prevailing turmoil, father and son do their part, as do so many others there.

After a few hours of celebrations and tributes, some people go wild, driven by the excess of drinks that are served generously.

Here and there, misunderstandings and excesses of all kinds are already breaking out, even among those who have daily confrontations but whom people believe to be saints.

Given the disturbance that is taking hold, father and son discreetly greet those closest to them and leave.

On the way home, Norbert does not hide his frustration. For some time now, he has not been able to get close to the one he loves.

He longs to be happy with the woman he loves, but between his intention and the realization of his desire, there is a reasonable distance that must be carefully measured.

To overcome the barriers it is necessary to take careful actions, as Brunilda will be the first victim of her father's fury.

The baron does not care at all about his daughter's feelings. Noticing his son, Wladimir abstains from commenting. Norbert will know what to do, when and how:

– "The world demands a lot from those who love, especially these days, given the present reality..."

As he reflects, swaying in the movements the vehicle makes, Wladimir takes a nap.

They finally arrive home. There is not much to say. They say goodbye and each goes off to carry out their more urgent interests.

Brunilda, in turn, regrets the distance created by circumstances between her and Norbert. She really loves the boy, but her father has already threatened to send her to a distant convent, under the care and surveillance of people he trusts, until she "gets well" and obeys the voice of reason. Faced with this, what to do? Danger surrounds her steps, and especially those of Norbert.

On the rare occasions when they spoke, they confirmed each other's interests, to the good fortune of her heart.

Her father; however, will not stop, not even for her feelings, not even for her safety.

What would Norbert say if he knew that her father had already beaten her? From those occasions physical and moral scars remained.

Many times, not even with Mina, her maid, does she manage to leave the house, but no matter what, she will never give up on Norbert. Without him, her life will be meaningless.

As she thinks concentrated, a servant unties her long golden hair, which falls in cascades, covering her. After the care that precedes the night's rest, in her nightgown, she admires the moon in its course; sometimes bright and silvery, fascinating with its light, sometimes hidden in the clouds, discreet...

She closes her eyes, thinks of Norbert and with passion and love remembers his image. Finally, she falls asleep.

Meanwhile, Norbert tosses and turns in bed, restless and sleepless.

– "What to do to satisfy his dearest longing?" – He thinks.

15.– THE BELOVED DAUGHTER

Minerva investigates the steps of Panderva, her "beloved daughter", while she tearfully tells those she meets in this search that has well defined intentions.

Wandering through the city in search of survival opportunities, she always seeks benefits she never earned and unthinkable privileges. To do so, she uses the talent of a failed actress and is always ready to stage the most convenient farce.

She has never seen Panderva since she escaped. Now; however, she must find her at all costs.

A few days ago, walking tirelessly through Florence, she rediscovered and revived old friendships.

In this way, she heard a rumor about a certain woman, from a noble and well-to-do family, who, ill with an incurable disease, is looking for someone who is very dear to her. When she knew who had started the rumor, she looked for her to find out more.

When they met, despite their mistrust, she and Berenice ended up understanding each other after all.

Increasingly enthusiastic about what they have experienced, the two narrate their own adventures, which led Berenice to confess something that left Minerva "ear perked up": a few years ago, she left a newborn baby girl in a miserable corner, by order of the mother herself, stating that she intended to rescue her during the night, but when she returned to the place, the girl was no longer there.

Suspicious, Minerva wanted to know more:

– Berenice, what did you want the baby for?

– To give her to my family!

– Would your family approve of your intention?

– Certainly, when I explained to them that we could later "charge" the mother for her shameful past! Of course, the expenses would far exceed what we could imagine! And so, we'd get our feet out of the mud!

Sighing, he lamented:

– But life decided otherwise and I never heard from that child again...! Today the mother, who is very ill, full of remorse, asks all the saints for the joy of knowing the whereabouts of her daughter!

Machiavellian as always, Minerva quickly saw it as a good opportunity:

– You worked for the Counts Alencar Nogueira for many years. Is this the arrogant Countess Carlota you are talking about?

– Exactly! The family has already spent a lot of money looking for the unfortunate girl! And I, who was asked that day to leave that little package anywhere, as long as she was far away, truncated my future plans! Life is very unfair!

– It certainly is! Do you remember the date when this happened?

– Yes! – Berenice tells her how, when and where, she left the child.

Minerva quickly concluded that that "little package" was her "beloved daughter", Panderva:

— "Look, look, how life is full of tricks! This treasure fell right into my hands and I ignored it for so many years! Good life, here I come! Panderva won't deny me this beautiful chance to be rich! She won't even dare to forget what she owes me...! That's why she was so rebellious! Her blood spoke louder...! She didn't even agree to do some "services" that would be so easy for her!
I need to find her, urgently...! "

— Are you fine, Minerva? – asked the other noticing her friend's silent reaction.

— I have never looked so fine, Berenice! I have never felt so good, believe me! Well, I have to go! Have a good time!

Hurriedly, she left her friend behind.

Knowing the address of the aforementioned family, Minerva began to look for them. However, they had moved to a more distant location.

With some effort and a lot of lies, she got the new address. Determined, she arrived at the residence and gained access to Count Fernando, whom she assured that she knew her granddaughter and where she was.

Radiant, he promised her benefits and a rich reward.

As Minerva ignores Panderva's whereabouts, she asks him for some time and warns him:

— Be careful, Count, I will ask you for a considerable sum! After all, I am as poor as Jacob! You understand me, don't you? – She rolls her eyes and shows a very sad face.

Although he was surprised by the insincerity and danger in that woman, he replied:

— I certainly understand! Bring my granddaughter and you won't regret it, I assure you!

— Then it's a deal! Wait for me!

Cyrene, once in the market, while picking fruit, overheard a strange conversation between two friends.

One of them was Berenice, who, having a big mouth as usual, told the same news she had told Minerva, adding:

– A few days ago, I ran into my friend, Minerva, after a long time! I thought it was great! Certainly, that hyena smells some advantage here...! Hum... She seemed too interested in the fact I just told you... Do you know the baby?

– Panderva! – adds the other –. And what a nice girl! She didn't even seem to be that witch's daughter!

In an enigmatic expression, Berenice completed:

– Maybe she wasn't, maybe she wasn't...! –. And she said no more. She packed her bags and left, very thoughtful.

Cyrene had never taken so long to choose what he wanted to buy. Dissimulated, he had listened to the conversation from beginning to end.

Once home, he told his boss everything.

– Excellent, Cyrene! God favors us, as always! Given this new fact, it will be easier to investigate Panderva's origin. Be attentive and let Forbes know! We know this woman very well from Panderva's narratives! Let her know that she needs to protect herself!

– Yes, sir!

Norbert's internal conflicts increase with each new day. He has already gained ground in the heart of the beautiful German woman and would spare no effort to have her. This was not the first and would not be the last couple to suffer reprisals simply for loving above human convention.

Love stories are often tragic, but it is impossible to prevent two hearts from attracting each other powerfully. It would be like trying to dam the waters of the ocean.

If life requires you to give up, what a sad fate will be yours...! You will live, if you survive, only by the force of circumstances!

These days, using a thousand tricks and with Percival's help, the lovers have met on some occasions.

At that moment, embraced and deeply involved in the same emotions, they exchange vows of love, forgetting the world and the real barriers that separate them.

Their friend Lucy, who helps Brunilda in these adventures, is currently collecting beautiful flowers in two baskets.

In the evening, the baron will receive the best flowers in his salons.

Kissing her, passionate and completely surrendered to his own emotions, Norbert holds Brunilda against his chest, when he hears two whistles.

It is Percival's sign.

Norbert embraces her and kisses her, almost desperate:

– Never forget that I love you more than myself!

Returning his caresses, she seeks strength within herself to let him go.

Releasing her, he begins to slowly pull away, but on impulse he rushes back, embraces her body with overwhelming passion and kisses her, completely devoted to this love. Every goodbye may be the last. Everything is uncertain, unpredictable...

Percival insists and repeats the sign.

Norbert looks into those eyes that bring the heavens and the earth closer to his soul, kisses them with reverence, while murmuring vows of love and, still holding her hand, slowly lets her go, without looking away from her... Gradually the distance increases, and Brunilda heads in the opposite direction.

As if in a dream, she receives the basket full of flowers from Lucy, while she watches Norbert's movements, smiling at him still in love and completely submissive to his love.

From a distance, Norbert bows to Lucy and makes a gesture of farewell and thanks to Percival.

Brunilda gets into her carriage and casts a last glance at him. Leaning against a tree, deep in despondency, Norbert watches them leave.

Little by little, the vehicle is only a small speck in the distance. Percival urges the horses to run wild. He fears that the delay will arouse "unfounded suspicions..." If this comes to pass, everyone will pay.

"How I would like to see this girl escape, in front of the baron's beard, to be happy with Norbert...!" – Percival wishes sincerely.

16.– COMFORTABLE AND WELL SERVED

Mr. Anastacio enjoys himself in his room, while with a sarcastic smile still remember the ridiculous images of those who, forgetting their own dignity, acted like docile little lambs, placing themselves at his feet...

Nevertheless, he rejected them. Each one really wanted to destroy him with his own hands...

Days later, refreshed from his journey and ready to meet the governors in Florence, he went to the various public, private and religious departments.

Everywhere, he could see the envious glances of men and the shameless interest of most of the women.

How could he resist that? It is extremely complicated to react against Nature and Nature was very generous, rewarding him with undeniable physical attributes...! His slightly bigger belly does not reduce his beauty. Proof of this is the fury with which the most important ladies dispute his company. Her voluptuous gaze makes his blood boil.

At that moment, his clerical robe spread out on the luxuriously upholstered chair. From his cuffs protrude valuable lace. Decorations and jewels complete the rich garment. After all, he must boast of the power he has.

His shiny and well-crafted shoes rest on an expensive Persian carpet and on the necklace that hangs from his neck the stones shine brilliantly.

The bulky and heavy cardinal's ring highlights the hand that dominates the profane world and at the same time represents his outstanding and undeniable performance in front of Holy Mother Church.

– "The representatives of the Lord must show their achievements in confirmation of the faith to the heavenly powers, so well directed by their priests...!" – He concludes, while dozing sometimes, without hiding his indifference to the endless meetings and sessions...

His valet touches his hand gently when he is about to fall clumsily from his seat.

Trembling, he pushes him violently, and gets up without caring about what is happening around him, in the tireless display of those who reveal their satisfaction of upsetting him, and sleepwalks through the endless corridors, making his servants run hurriedly after him, to attend to him in his regal room.

Upon arrival, he throws himself on a bed under a rich canopy and promptly falls asleep.

The servant sighs in annoyance and foresees the effort he will have to make to remove his garments and all the ornaments, in order to prepare him for his rest.

If he does not do so, he will have to resist inevitable punishments.

As long as his sleep lasts, he should tell those who seek him that His Eminence the Cardinal is away at important meetings. Since these are secret, no one will receive proper directions. And who would even dare to doubt his words?

Panderva appears and Cyrene tells her that his boss wants to talk to her.

Quickly, she goes to him:

– Did you call me, good man? – She asks anxiously.

– Yes, my dear friend! We heard that Minerva is nearby and is looking for you.

– I know... She hasn't seen me yet, but I have already seen her terrifying figure! Minerva brought me only pain and misery!

Apparently dejected, she sits down.

– Do not be like that, Panderva!

– And how should I feel? She hasn't given up living off me yet! May God take her away!

– Calm down, please, and listen...

He tells her everything he knows about her probable origins. Panderva listens to all he has to say.

Pale and misty-eyed, she reveals remarkable anxiety and much emotion.

Wladimir calls Cyrene and asks him for a glass of water. After drinking it, calmer, she listens to Wladimir:

– Minerva is most likely already taking the lead.

– Yes, she is very quick when she sees the possibility of profit and benefits!

– We have to organize ourselves to keep her away! Could you help us?

Fearful, Panderva asks:

– What could I do?

– Nothing so difficult, believe me. You will have to look for her and give her a note! Do you agree?

– Yes! I will do whatever you ask me to do...

– When you see Minerva, stay alert and do not expose yourself too much!

– Do not worry! I am no longer that girl she once subjugated!

Wladimir observes strong feelings of rejection.

– Have you forgiven Minerva?

– I do not know... I have very sad memories of my life with her... She left a deep impression on me... However, I keep asking myself:

And what will she herself have received from life? Won't her malice be the result of sufferings equal to mine? I am very sorry for those who, like her, hurt and hurt her... Imbued with these thoughts, I will be able to forgive her, little by little...

– Wise friend! Someday we will understand our fellow man, driven by a healthy empathy!

Laughing, excited, Panderva declares:

– Kind man already does this, certainly!

– I struggle, Panderva, for reverence to God and solidarity with man! Anyway, do you want protection when you talk to Minerva?

– We know this is not practical, because she will expect me to be alone.

– I agree, we are, however, at your disposal! If you need help and defense, inform us!

– Thank you! I will know how to keep a reasonable distance, do not worry!

Wladimir hands her a note for Minerva and says:

– May heaven protect you!

– You and your son too...!

Wladimir is very pleased with Panderva's deference to Norbert. She leaves and he, wrapped up in work, papers, documents, requests and appointments, sees another night coming...

The stars are already twinkling in vain in the sky when Norbert arrives home.

There is no need to ask where he comes from, because the sparkle in his eyes and a few wrinkles on his forehead speak louder than words.

They greet each other, have dinner together and go to their respective rooms.

Norbert longs for privacy. He wants to expand the glorious moments of his love.

His chest barely contains his heart that beats fast at the mere memory of Brunilda. For her and for this love, he will do anything! She comes first, then life itself!

Percival and Lucy have been great friends. Without their good will and tricks, they could never enjoy the moments of incomparable love and affection, which glorify their own life at its best.

The next day, the baron will host a grand banquet, and his daughter – oh, misfortune...! – is the main reason for this event: beautiful, cultured, intelligent and good, she attracts glances, desires and great ambitions.

Norbert knows how the baron "educates" his daughter. His cruelty knows no bounds and his actions border on madness: "Exposed to so many eyes and offered as merchandise...!"

Norbert jumps out of bed and begins to pace restlessly. Thoughts like these torment his soul, day by day.

When she succumbs to her father's authority, what will it be like? He shudders at the possibility of losing her and worst of all: to know that she is unhappy!

Wladimir imagines and regrets his son's torments.

No man who truly loves can avoid suffering, especially when situations are very adverse ... He supports his son, for her and for this love.

Little by little, finally, he falls asleep.

Meanwhile, Norbert reflects on himself and the situation he is currently living:

– ""I need to find a way out! I have never really loved and when I do it, I face this crazy impossibility...! Now I understand the desperate actions of those who loved and faced dangers and the world itself to live their love or die for it...! Love! Divine feeling and conductor of souls, ultimate happiness for any human being on this controversial and unstable planet, collector and mixture of good and evil, joys and sorrows, pains and glorious achievements...!

"We sleep and wake up every day. It is great when we love and are loved!" – He concludes, before falling asleep, overwhelmed by the fatigue of the day and night.

Panderva goes to the same places where she has always lived and makes a comparison between who she was and who she is. It is impossible to reconcile the two ways of life, starting with her appearance and continuing with her current social behavior...

Those who maintained a relation with her, today look at her with distrust and, despite the feeling of loss that grips her, she understands them; she has been like that and has acted like them too...

"What will God have reserved for all of us? Only He can know..." – She reflects without revealing animosity towards the rejections she suffers from those who used to vibrate with her friendly presence.

For now, she feels somewhat lost; time has passed changing her, and the one to come is a great unknown...

You cannot, nor should you, desire excessive wealth, luxury and comfort:

"I predict that my life will change and this frightens me! The fraternal support of the Vladosks has been a preamble for the next stages of my life. With them, I gradually became better and more tolerant, more grateful and wiser... The gentleman who is looking for me can be a bridge between this reality and another one that I do not know yet... Reason warns me of the dangers that he represents, but I feel a strong inclination to respond to his wishes... Intuition tells me that we both have issues to resolve. However, I have a great fear of failure..."

Thus wrapped up in intimate thoughts and having her little dog as her only companion, she asks:

– We are alone, aren't we, my friend? Those who come to us today do it only to take advantage!

The animal barks as he runs to catch up with her, stopping here and there to sniff out what interests him.

Suddenly he stops, growls menacingly and starts barking stridently.

Panderva looks around and easily understands his reaction. He had already seen Minerva.

She hides in fear. Her heart was beating wildly as he remembered how many times that little animal had defended her from Minerva's blows and had been equally beaten in his uncontrollable rage.

She has to talk to her, but she cannot! She feels a great aversion for her... However, she promised to deliver the gentleman's message...

She comes out of her hiding place very frightened.

Minerva, who has been looking for her in every possible and imaginable corner, shouts loudly:

– Ah, there you are! I need to talk to you! Despite the "disguise" you are wearing, I recognized you! Where did you get that costume?

Realizing that passersby are listening to her, she changes her speech:

– Please, my daughter, listen to me! I have so much to tell you! After all, I raised you with such dedication, didn't I?

Panderva remains silent.

Minerva approaches and with every step she takes, Panderva shudders.

Minerva reaches for her, tries to hug her, but she jumps back, defending herself and keeping her guard up.

– What happens, my daughter? Don't you recognize me anymore?

– What do you want?

– Me? I want you to come with me to meet someone! That is all!

Keeping her guard up, Panderva replies:

– No, I am not going anywhere with you! But I have a message for you that will interest you a lot!

– Coming from you, I doubt it very much!

– You can trust! Look, in this document there is an address of someone very important you can talk to! It is the best for you, I assure you!

Panderva hands her the paper; distrustful, she takes a look at it and is surprised, she remains silent. She keeps it inside her clothes and exclaims mockingly and aggressively, while surrounding the girl, analyzing her appearance:

– Ah...! You did well, eh? And alone, without sharing with me, ungrateful! What else can I expect from you? Just that...!

Minerva begins a performance and laments, forgetting that Panderva knows this theater very well...

Seeing that she could not deceive her as she expected, she exclaims applauding:

– You are worthy of applause! Anyway, you managed to get up in life! Hum... Everything you are wearing is of good quality! And this perfume? What a jewel! But as you can see, I am still in misery and you do not even care, do you? But when "your man" finds out about your ingratitude, he will surely throw you out on the street, where you should have stayed! And on second thought, what are you doing here, killing nostalgia for the good old days?

As she speaks, treacherously, she rushes towards Panderva and snatches the small silk bag she is carrying, from which the girl has taken the paper with the address.

She moves away and investigates the interior of the accessory, rejoicing:

– Ah, there is money here, it is mine now, and don't you dare confront me! – She says, throwing angry glances at Panderva, who is running away.

Meanwhile, Minerva counts the coins Forbes gave Panderva for services provided in the kitchen.

She squints her ugly little eyes and mumbles ambitiously:

– Well, well, "daughter", there must be more where they came from...!

Reddened by the rush, Panderva arrives at Vladosk's house after having gone several different routes to avoid being followed by Minerva.

Trembling, she can barely speak. After so long, she was once again confronted with her past of pain, deprivation, beatings and total insecurity.

In these moments, the distance between this time and the time that has passed can be valued and measured.

Calm down, tell them what happened.

Cyrene and Forbes console her in every way. She, however, dodges them and looks for her room to cry...

17.– THE AGREEMENT

With the address Panderva gave her, Minerva overdresses and presents herself at the Provincial Court. Very curious, she has similar thoughts and intentions to her cruel way of being and living.

Still climbing the steps of the building, she encounters a guard who soon stands in her way, chasing her away:

– Back off, woman! What could someone like you want here? Get out of here!

With her hands on her hips and her face reddened with anger, she glares at him and replies:

– Let me pass! I know why I came and what for!

Then, from the bag she had stolen from Panderva, she takes the signed and sealed note made by Wladimir Vladosk, and shows it defiantly:

– Can you read? Then read! Look at the document I have in my hands and which is addressed to me, "Minerva"!

He examines it but still hesitates. Exasperated, she pulls the shawl she wears over her shoulders and boldly asks:

– So, what then? Are you going to talk to your superior? If you want, go confirm, I will wait for you! Know that I am woman of class and I never lie!

But resolve it soon, otherwise you will make me waste my time!

Grimacing, he puts the order away, he may need it later. He steps away and allows her to pass.

Minerva enters the building, when she hears:

– *Strega...*![5]

She turns around and curses him:

– If I were one of those, I would turn you into a pretty filthy rat right now!

Superstitious, he fights back:

– I conjure you...! –. He makes a cross with his fingers, crosses himself several times and kisses the cross around his neck.

Minerva is very satisfied with the fear she caused. Inside the building, she looks at everything with eyes of prey.

In front of Wladimir's office, she tries to enter, but the person in charge of organizing access orders her to sit down and wait.

– You want me to sit down? That is not why I came here! Mr. Wladimir Vladosk called me and I cannot waste my time!

Frowning, the employee repeats the imperative:

– Sit down! When your turn comes, you will be called!

– if you are not aware, my dear sir, I am here for a very important appointment!

Ignoring her, the man walks away, while in front of the waiting bench she pushes those already seated and struggles for a seat, while thinking about the possibility of approaching them to ask for money. Smiling mischievously, she remembers when she needed to pinch Panderva to make her cry to move the passersby.

---

[5] Witch.

– "Today the ingrate dresses well and even has money! I need to know where she lives! She owes me a lot and she will have to pay me back! – she says.

Slowly, she leans her head and, almost falls out of her seat, snoring loudly and disturbing everyone.

Late in the afternoon, she wakes up, stretches and asks:

– After all, how long am I going to wait here? Who will pay me for the time I am wasting? I need to talk to Mr. Wladimir Vladosk!

She scratches her head, sighs and goes out into the corridors whining. Some, hearing her complaints, sincerely repent, while she continues to narrate her misfortunes: how poor she is, how much she suffers, how many children she has to feed…! Only God knows her sorrows and sleepless nights...!

Some people take coins out of their pockets and give them to her.

Finally, the moment she was waiting for arrives. She will be received. She enters the office, slithering like a treacherous snake.

Meanwhile, Wladimir examines her, careful and silent, lamenting her spiritual misery.

– Sit down! – He says politely.

– Again? I want to know why you called me! Ah! I also came because I want you to explain about my dear daughter!

– Who is your "dear daughter"?

– Well, well, why do you ask me questions as if you didn't know her? Who else would cover her with silks and lace? This is as clear as water...! Well, you have to know she has a mother!

– Please, madam, stop talking in riddles! Accusations like these can put you in jail in the blink of an eye! Look where you are and do not act without thinking!

Frightened, Minerva keeps silent and contains herself. Intimately, she ponders how to spend a few days in prison. She has long known the "comfort" offered by filthy cells.

Wladimir tells her sternly:

– I am going to ask you some questions. Answer carefully and be very honest: Who is looking for Panderva, why and what for?

Rolling her eyes, she declares:

– Ah, I can tell you that, it is a secret that does not belong to me!

Looking at her seriously, Wladimir repeats the same question.

Silence…

– I just need confirmation, because in fact I already know about everything!

She suddenly stands up and answers:

– How treacherous are men of law! You are always looking for ways to hurt us or put us in jail!

Sighing, she sits down again and explains:

– The one who is looking for her is the mother who is sick and wants to see her! I told you I am her mother and that is true too, because I am her foster mother!

– Since when?

– Since her first day of life!

– And who gave you Panderva?

– A friend of mine.

– Where did he bring the newborn from?

– How would I know? He dumped the load on me and he was drunker than a skunk!

– Now, you are looking for Panderva because new facts have come to the fore, right?

– Yes! Her real mother, as I was saying, appeared and she already knows that her daughter stayed there, where I have always lived!

– How did she know?

– At that time, her maid, Berenice, was my friend. She was the one who "dropped off" the child in our alley. She intended to pick her up later, but that friend of mine arrived earlier. Panderva must be the same child!

– And what is your interest in this?

– What a question! Are you forgetting that I am her foster mother?
The family is very rich and they promised me a good reward!

As she analyzes her lines, she continues:

– Panderva's mother is dying. She's repentant, she wants to apologize to the daughter!

– You are, for now, the only point of reference the family has, right?

– Yes, I am!

– And why did your friend Berenice want the child?

– She intended to hide her and let time pass. In the future, she would extort money from the real mother to improve her life!

– Improve her life through extortion? Dishonest and criminal! She could be condemned!

Standing up and mockingly swaying she explains her philosophy of life:

– Honesty, my lord, is for those who have money! Among us, honesty finds no room! We have learned that every day and in the hardest way imaginable...! Come live with us and you will understand many things...!

– Although what you say has some basis, madam, poverty does not fatally lead to dishonesty! It may lead to sufferings, but these can serve, in turn, as a stimulus to the strength and courage to fight for oneself, without becoming corrupt! Those who persevered in doing good, especially in adversity, left great examples for our humanity. The greatest one: "the Son of Man had nowhere to rest his head...!"

Bored with what she considers a tedious litany, she reveals her impatience:

– Very well! You have made your speech! What more do you want from me?

– To know what your intentions are!

– Why do you ask me that? I will take Panderva to her mother and I will get the reward! Then we will all be very happy! But what did you call me for? So far you have talked, talked and nothing! What do you want anyway?

– I want to make a deal with you! – Cunningly, she answers:

– I am interested... Come on, what's this all about?

– I want you to get out of Panderva's life completely!

– Right now? Oh, I get it! You want to keep everything, don't you? That must be it! Will you take the bread out of my mouth? But then, are you an "important man" in this Court? – she asks defiantly.

Wladimir looks at her with great pity, and concludes, "This woman, like so many others, is the sad result of the world's misery and unlove... They react with the resources they know to survive..."

To his silence, she exclaims directly:

– So, are you going to tell me what you really want or not?

– Listen to me and consider the deal I want to offer you: leave Panderva alone and I will reward you!

Without hesitation, she replies:

– I do not see how! Do you want to prevent me from receiving the reward I was promised?

– I will know the value of the promised amount and I will give it to you. So, do you agree? This way, they will not hurt you.

– Hum... I do not know... You have many ways to fool me! I can fall for one of those...!

– As you can see, I have a name and a position to take care of! I would never fool anyone! I guarantee it!

However, I warn you to stay away from the case and Panderva forever. From now on, only the law will handle this case and you have no ties to her, as you are not, in fact, her real mother.

Clenching her evil and ambitious eyes, she looks at Wladimir and asks, very intrigued:

– Now it is I who want to know: what is your interest in all this?

– The interest is not mine, but hers and her family's! I already have the case in my hands!

Minerva sighs, walks around the room, and shows a lot of hesitation.

Wladimir waits for her to accept without unreasonable demands. She thinks, thinks and finally declares:

– All right! I will do as you ask! But I will keep my guard up! You will not fool me!

– No one will fool you, I said. And as for "keeping your guard up," give up! The girl in question needs protection from you! Don't challenge your luck! If she is questioned, you will be seriously compromised by the law!

Minerva nods silently.

She decides to quickly take advantage of his goodwill, before he decides to pursue legal means to get what he wants and let her with nothing.

– When will I get paid?

– When I know the value! The payment will be made right here!

– All right! Do not try to fool me, I know how to be pretty mean when I want to!

Wladimir almost smiles at such a misguided provocation... When Minerva leaves, he lets out a sigh of relief.

Her dear friend Panderva will soon have her identity, last name and address rescued. No doubt this will make your heart very happy...

18.– METAPHYSICS

Immersed in his scientific theses, Wladimir analyzes the natural evolution of the Earth, present and future.

As a man of faith, he rationally concludes the presence and power of the Creator.

He enthusiastically admires those who have brought relevant knowledge to the world. Many have gone to the ultimate consequences in the name of Truth. Some have left their names in history and many others have become anonymous, but they consciously incline to the transcendent and eternal, rather than to the brevity of material existence.

On the other hand, many others followed the path of error and falsehood, out of fear or interest.

Divine perfection is a fact proved by reason and heart; yet many who claim to be representatives of heaven vehemently deny this perfection, exchanging sacred benefits that hover over human conventions and their weaknesses.

Yet those who see the Truth and strive for the observance of the Law, with admirable examples of love and faith, are persecuted and stigmatized.

Wladimir, concentrated, did not even notice his son approaching. In patent adoration and with an air of admiration, Norbert smiles silently.

Turning around, he surprises him.

Still reflective, he hands him the handwritten sheets. Norbert receives them and sits down to read.

In silence, he devours each line to the end. He is an undisputed admirer of his dad's wisdom.

A few moments later, he stands with the papers in his hands and smiles as he comments:

– If your persecutors had access to this, they would have much to celebrate!

Laughing as well, Wladimir agrees:

– I know, but what can I do, I need to think, to investigate, to deduce, to understand life! For this, the Creator has endowed me with intelligence!

He takes a few steps, restless, and declares with an almost theatrical emphasis, as if he were in the forum defending his causes:

– Norbert, I am exultant before so much greatness! The different sciences seduce me, attract me, viscerally! They are part of my life! I could never live without analyzing the world and all that surrounds me in depth! Besides our little planet, I also ask about others, as they gravitate in space, under the natural and perfect laws!

One day we were there and sooner or later we will return to many of them to live new experiences. It is only a matter of time! They are celestial abodes equal, worse or better than this one where we toil, day by day, in the fulfillment of a powerful and unquestionable will that commands everything!

And so many other things invite me to investigate, discover, assimilate, in a vast and endless learning process!

We are gods and we can do anything if we know how to make good use of these powers, even ignored or despised, labeled as miraculous, superstitions, witchcraft and so many other adjectives that reveal the incompetence of men to label what they do not know, because they do not strive to know, and while they are simply satisfied with what our little world offers, "they do not enter or let enter heaven!"

Poor miserable ones, sooner or later, they will feel the regret of delaying Truth on the planet, of which, they think themselves masters!

Blind, lazy, proud and selfish, traitors to true science and traitors to divine power!

He walks almost forgetting where he is and asks:

– What reassures us? Knowing that everyone, without exception, will one day understand all that they deny today for convenience. Time, implacable, immune to our influence, continues indifferent and with it comes the vehicle of legitimate progress that passes, invisible and invincible, over everything and everyone, transforming and perfecting the existing.

Those who have long been the champions of good and justice on this planet will continue to fight for good and truth in all their lives, likewise, many of those who manipulate truth for their own benefit will one day be giving their own lives for it; happy and fulfilled, in spite of the pains and sufferings they will go through to correct their past mistakes!

Have we prevented many from following their own paths? We shall be bridges of light, allowing them new and blessed opportunities!

Wladimir takes a breath, raises his arms and exclaims in conclusion:

– Finally, we will always be right with our conscience in the eyes of the Law!

The science that synthesizes in itself the truth of love and reason is the philosopher's stone and all alchemy!

With his face flushed with euphoria and enthusiasm, Wladimir sits down again and takes a deep breath, calms down, nods once more time:

– You are right, here – he shows the sheets – they would find everything they need to take me to the torments of Tartarus!

Hugging him by the shoulders, excited and reverent, Norbert exclaims:

– But above the will of our enemies, may divine providence watch over you, my father!

– Over us, my son, over us!

Changing the subject, he asks:

– Tell me, son, if you can and if you want: what have you done about your feelings?

Norbert gets more comfortable and tells him, laughing and serious at the same time, the adventures he has been undertaking to see his beloved and the times he embraced her, kissed her and enjoyed the happiness of being loved.

– And how did you accomplish this?

– With her consent, the help of her friend Lucy and also the coachman Percival. He likes me and that is why he decided to help us.

– De *motu propio*, eh?

– Yes, fortunately!

After hours of pleasant conversations, Wladimir puts his documents away and leaves, hugging his son.

They sit down at the dinner table and eat a relaxed meal. Before retiring to their rooms, Wladimir said to him:

– By an admirable chance, if there is such a thing, we apparently discovered the family of Panderva. I have already taken charge of everything. Cyrene and Forbes have been helping us. However...

– However...?

– We cannot even imagine what she could face if she really belonged to that family!

– Why do you say that, my father?

– Listen... –. Wladimir told him the name of Panderva's possible grandfather.

– You are right... Poor child, in spite of her moral values, has countless compromises with her past.

– That is right, my son. I fear for the future of our dear friend. What's to come?

– She can always count on us!

Saddened, Wladimir asks:

– And how can we know what awaits us too? Life offers us opportunities to do well! How, when and where?

– It is true... I believe that Panderva will now face the challenges that wealth and power bring. I hope she has enough strength to resist! Ever since she was born, her life has been a painful lesson in humility!

– Yes! May she have strength...!

19.– CONVIVIENCE

In Forbes' room, comfortably lying on a soft bed, Panderva dreams with her eyes open.

It is impossible for her not to remember, moved, the interest of this gentleman who speaks to her heart more than he should.

Mesmerized, she sighs.

At the moment, she is physically tired. Currently she supports Forbes as much as she can. The kindly man was right; she is overtired and aging. What keeps her working at home is the love she feels for her bosses and the fear of changing her life. She wouldn't get used to anywhere else. Wladimir's house today is also her home.

Now, with Panderva's help, Forbes can rest, especially when her tenacious rheumatism torments her, because the young woman takes control of everything, saving her the work.

Before falling asleep, Panderva reflects on how good her life is there.

Very grateful, Forbes, from time to time, rewards her with some coins, which she receives and appreciates.

Gradually, Panderva became calmer, more polite and, above all, less impetuous.

In the next few days she will meet a family that could be hers. She is afraid of what is to come, but she will be accompanied by Cyrene and Forbes.

In addition, an official of the Provincial Court will represent the good man.

20.– COUNT FERNANDO

Quickly, Wladimir sent an officer with a letter to the head of Panderva's presumed family, after all, according to the news, her mother is dying.

The next day, he receives in his office a visit from a prissy, elegant, gray-haired man.

Impatient, he introduces himself and inquires:

– I am Count Fernando de Alencar Nogueira! What do you want?

– Please sit down! – Wladimir tells him.

– Please, for what purpose was I summoned to this court?

– Take it easy and listen: I have received information about an acquaintance that seriously involves your family. I decided to call you to find out the truth.

– From whom did you receive this information?

– I cannot tell you!

– If you tell me what it is about...

– I heard that your daughter was very ill and was looking for someone whose whereabouts she did not know.

Taking a deep breath, the man finally explains his situation, his daughter's illness and her consequent anxiety to find her daughter, of whom the family itself has always ignored the existence.

When he finishes his narration, he cries without shame. He wipes his tears and concludes:

– Anyway, that's it!

Wladimir keeps silent. In front of him stood a father weeping for his beloved daughter, oblivious to his surroundings.

Noticing Wladimir's calm and understanding, he opens his heart:

– My daughter has rare moments of lucidity, and in those moments she always begs to see the daughter she abandoned... When she is asked how this happened, she declares that she counted on the complicity of her servant, Berenice, who left the child in the first dark and deserted alley she found... Since then she has never heard from her daughter, who must now be a young girl. Do you know anyone who matches this information?

– Everything leads me to believe it!

– I wish I could relieve my dear daughter's physical and moral pains! Who is it about? I know you would not call me if you did not have reliable information!

– Reliable, but not yet proven!

– You would be surprised how many times we go places and end up disappointed. Every new day we have new hopes that lead to failure.

– Cases like this are numerous and the paths taken are no exception to the usual mishaps. The information I have should be analyzed by your family and the one you are looking for.

– You mentioned an acquaintance...

– Yes. And she could be the granddaughter you are looking for!

Surprised, the count can barely speak.

– Once the official investigations are concluded, we intend to bring you together, if you wish.

Fernando, who had stood up, sat down again, dealing with his obvious physical weakness, such was his emotion.

– That's all I want most, dear sir!

After agreeing on the date and time of Panderva's visit, as well as the conditions for it, Panderva's presumed grandfather takes his leave:

– I will be there! Today as never before I am far from home... I do not know when the heavens will take my daughter away forever...!

Hurriedly, he exclaims before leaving:

– I will be at your disposal! I await you with great anticipation, as you can imagine.

He reaches out and shakes Wladimir's hand. Almost at the door, he turns around and asks an emotional question:

– Do you have children?

– Yes! A son who is the biggest reason for my existence!

– Then, I hope you do not judge me and understand me. I am not and have never been a good role model for my daughter and I am aware of that. This is the part that torments me the most. If I were different, she would have the courage to tell me her life experiences and today, who knows, she would not be dying full of remorse! I know about you from what people say! Your life is an open book! Honor and dignity are your standards! However, above and beyond the circumstances, at this moment, here we are just two parents who love their children!

– I respect their pain and do not judge others, except in terms of my profession. Human beings are much more complex than we imagine! However, when we learn to love all God's creatures, as we love our own, we will all be happy...!

– I see no possibilities for this, forgive me! I know; however, that I am in the presence of a wise man of indisputable values! Therefore, as I have no adequate allegations to contradict your assertion, I limit myself to thanking you for your attention! Have a good day...!

– Have a good day! You will soon receive a visit from my protégée!

He puts his hat back on and leaves, crestfallen and thoughtful.

After saying goodbye, Wladimir remains standing and reflects:

"Above our imperfections, whatever they may be, we love, whether it be a loved one, a little animal, a place, an object... If we were born to love, when will we realize it...?"

He sits down and prepares to continue with the day's activities.

21.– MOTHER AND DAUGHTER

Panderva is very excited to meet Count Fernando's family.

– Minerva finally left her alone, she did not even know where to find her. –.

Nervous, she has cried several times and cannot concentrate on anything.

She chose a beautiful dress with Forbes' help, who asked her with tears in his eyes:

– My daughter, please, if life takes you out of here, do not forget about us, okay?

Silently, she hugged her tightly, grateful and moved... There had never been anyone who loved her like that.

Cyrene intervenes humorously:

– Forbes, thank God for being able to get rid of the job this girl gives you!

Angrily, Forbes replies:

– Don't say that, Cyrene! Today I don't know how to live without her anymore!

– I know, friend... I was just joking... – he concludes equally excited.

Panderva would not like to be without her friends... They are so good, sincere, kind...

She hides the tears that are starting to fall and heads to the backyard, where her four-legged friend currently lives in a beautiful little house made just for him. He is chubby and already likes Forbes, so sometimes he gets spoiled a bit...

Panderva sits on a bench with the little dog on her lap and tries to imagine the near future.

However, after a few minutes, she wipes away his tears, raises his head and exclaims bravely:

– The future is God's! May he guide me!

The next day, she leaves with Cyrene, Forbes and the official representative of Wladimir Vladosk.

They drive through the city by carriage and gradually leave the urban perimeter behind them.

After a considerable time, they see the rich residence that impresses for its beauty and magnificence. With a beautiful farmhouse, everything in it reveals that it is a cosmopolitan residence.

After the illness of the countess, and to benefit her in various treatments, the family decided to live there.

Following several boulevards with lush gardens and orchards, the carriage drives around the portentous building and parks.

The porter, who was already waiting for them, nodded to the coachman, indicating a place in front of the facade, where all the servants in charge of welcoming them gathered.

Cyrene and Forbes, very well dressed, bow. Identifying himself, the representative of the Provincial Court declares that the visit will be supervised by him and properly recorded in official papers. However, he will leave all arrangements to Cyrene and Forbes.

Finally, they enter the luxurious residence.

Panderva, target of everyone's curiosity, feels overwhelmed by so much financial power and labels. If only she had the courage to run away from there, leaving everything behind. Pale and trembling, her eyes blurred with tears.

For unknown reasons, she feels in her own soul the pain of that house and the weight of its sorrows.

She has been told that her presumed mother is very ill.

In the days prior to the visit, she prepared herself to confirm, or not, her bond with that family. If this is confirmed, fully and unquestionably, his life will change inexorably from one moment to the next.

He steps carefully on the floor polished with chromatic colors, result of an exquisite geometric work.

All around her, the realization of wealth in every possible and imaginable form, in the visual display of financial power.

At that moment, she struggles like a fish out of water, between the life she knows through experience and what her past and future hold.

What measures do you have to assess these two realities?! Only subjectivity.

Yes, she cannot deny it. Everything she sees attracts her, irresistibly, though she would like to deny such a dangerous attraction.

Forbes understands her conflicts and hugs her by the shoulders, while whispering affectionately:

– Calm down, Panderva, and don't rush! Give life some time until the different situations ease up, becoming more comprehensible. However, from now on, rest your soul, I am sure no one will shame you!

Nodding her head in approval, she wipes away her tears and lets out a sob.

– Forbes, Forbes! My good friend! Why did I get myself into this? I shouldn't have been looking for what I have lost for so long!

– You are wrong, daughter, you should! If it were not so, the gentleman himself would never have consented to this meeting, nor would he have done all he could for this day to come!

Hearing the reference to her good friend, Panderva takes a deep breath and decides to be grateful for all the help she is receiving.

Meanwhile, the owner of the house approached solicitously and deeply moved:

– Welcome to my house! – He exclaims.

Then, he searches Panderva's face with his eyes and cannot hide his astonishment, as he becomes pale and stumbles.

One of the servants runs to his aid, given his unusual reaction.

Fernando immediately recognized, in Panderva's features, his own daughter in the golden age.

In a barely audible voice, he whispers:

– Not only do they look alike, they are identical...!

Finally in a better state, he addresses the guests:

– I greet you all, thanking you, from now on, for your presence and effort to accept our invitation. I am Count Fernando, owner of the house. Make yourselves comfortable! May I know your names?

– Certainly! – answers the officer, while handing him a document – I am Sosthenes, representative of the Provincial Court and, as you know, I am at the service of Mr. Wladimir Vladosk!

Those accompanying me are Mr. Cyrene, Ms. Forbes and the young Panderva!

– Panderva... Strange name...– he murmurs intrigued. Delicate, she defends herself:

– I think so too, but I learned to like my name! – Meanwhile, she carefully examines the man who may be her grandfather.

Still not fully recovered from the first emotion, Fernando shudders as he comments once again, very excited:

– Your voice...!

Curious, Panderva wants to know:

– Have you heard my voice before, sir?

Quickly realizing that he once again let emotion take over his usual rationality, Fernando explains:

– No, no! I have never heard your voice before! Forgive my sudden outbursts! I am not usually like this, but I am completely amazed at the resemblance between you and my daughter Carlota! It's as if she had re-emerged from the past! Even your voice is like your mother's!

Despite wanting to remain neutral in order to rationally analyze the facts, this statement moved Panderva more than expected, and she had to control herself not to cry.

Determined, Fernando invited them with broad gestures to follow him:

– Come please! All the time is precious! My daughter is now lucid and able to understand us! Today is surprisingly good. She accepted all the care for her bath!

Panderva's heart beats wildly. In a few moments she will face someone who could be her real mother.

Those who accompany her are equally moved. They walk down long corridors and after a while they approach a room, which at the entrance smells of medicines and herbal aromas.

The atmosphere is sad and morbid, despite the luxury and comfort.

Little by little they see a woman lying and panting, on top of a bed covered by a canopy, which receives the faint light of the stained-glass windows. She reveals a great curiosity for those who have just entered.

Panderva can no longer hide her excitement.

Afraid of weakening, her restless and anxious soul desires to decipher the past...

Hesitant and fearful, she accepts the hand of Fernando, who leads her carefully and expectantly to Carlota's bed.

In front of this unfortunate woman, bathed in sweat, breathing with extreme difficulty and revealing great anxiety in her eyes, she confirms Fernando's statements regarding their physical similarity.

Addressing his daughter, Fernando says:

– Dear, look, this may be the daughter you have been looking for for so long, look how alike you are! Given the investigations we made, the greatest possibility fell on this girl!

Carefully scrutinizing her facial features, unmeasured emotions seized her heart, in sacred recognition of her beloved daughter, Carlota confirms:

– Yes, she is my daughter! – She responds with effort, while extending her hands, in an attempt to attract Panderva.

Panderva approaches wrapped in an emotion that almost suffocates her and lets herself be touched by Carlota's cold, wet hands. In that touch, an indefinable feeling reaches her, as if it were possible to remember her...

Fernando explains:

– My daughter told us about the drama she was going through, a long time later, when she no longer had any point of reference in this regard. Since then, she lives for this moment!

Carlota's almost faded voice is heard:

– I am sorry... my daughter...!

Panderva asks her curiously:

– Do you really believe that I am your daughter?

– My heart recognizes you! Yes, you are my daughter...!

Panderva never imagined herself in such a situation.

At this point, Fernando cries convulsively and tears begin to flow from the eyes of the others. Even the officer so accustomed to similar has tears in his eyes.

Despite her physical weakness, Carlota squeezes Panderva's hand as she cries.

Respectfully, Panderva kisses her hands.

Almost without strength and speaking with difficulty, Carlota asks:

– Daughter, give me a hug and forgive me for everything... I need your forgiveness!

Making a great effort to hold back her tears and express herself, Panderva says with affection:

– I have nothing to forgive, my mother, because I also need divine forgiveness! Only Heaven can judge us correctly and I would never be disgraceful! I certainly received from life what I deserved and needed!

Overwhelmed, Panderva hugs her against her own heart. She seems to have lived this sacred and solemn moment...

Thus embraced, they remain.

Time seems ecstatic, and joins with benevolence to the reunion of these two hearts.

The emotion, however, exhausted the patient, making her feel worse. The doctors who were also watching the touching scene rushed to her aid.

Panderva knows that this is her last moment and deeply regrets her sufferings...

Before leaving, she approaches her and whispers in her ear:

– I will stay here, rest! As soon as I can, I will see you again! Be at peace! Rest your heart and know that my soul recognizes yours. We are, above all, mother and daughter!

Smiling, in a Herculean effort, Carlota moans and begins to writhe in the sheets.

Forbes, deeply compassionate, embraces Panderva. Outside, Panderva lets her emotions flow and cries convulsively, needing help.

She goes to the garden where she sits on a comfortable bench. She takes a deep breath and tries to calm herself. A maid brings her hot tea, which she gratefully drinks.

* * *

In her bed when the unbearable pains threatened to cloud her reasoning; anticipating the visit of the one who, sooner or later, leads everyone along the paths of the spirit, Carlota abandoned forever her earthly fantasies and ambitions and courageously decided to face her own mistakes, especially that of hidden and renegade motherhood...

Knowing that she would soon leave the earth, she decided to confess her sins, first to the Church, as dictated by the precepts of her religion, and then to her father, who, given her tragic fate, would not have the courage to judge and condemn her.

Always spoiled in excess, very rich and owner of an admirable beauty – although without a moralized education – and living with deplorable examples, she behaved irresponsibly and some time later she was pregnant.

The shock was great and led her to fear the wrath of her family, especially her father.

She decided and planned to get rid of the one who threatened to disgrace her in front of everything and everyone.

On a long journey, accompanied by her most faithful servant and far from home, she waited for the right moment.

Before giving birth, she came back and found refuge in the house of a trusted friend, far away from her family.

After many hours of suffering and doubts about whether or not she would survive, she heard her daughter's first cries. For some moments, her mother's heart was moved, but controlling herself, she rejected the sacred feeling of motherhood and ordered Berenice to take her away.

She only heard that she was a beautiful and strong girl...

Thus, the little being, wrapped in cloth, was abandoned in a place of difficult access, in a nearby neighborhood.

For Carlota, everything seemed to be solved.

When the time passed, more blushed and apparently well, she returned home, telling about supposed incidents experienced during the trip.

Years passed and she tried to forget about her rejected daughter. But when all seemed forgotten, she became so ill that she could not get out of bed.

In the midst of countless different treatments, she became discouraged. She no longer believed in a cure.

Losing the vigor that used to characterize her, she was consumed by painful remorse, condemning herself in torment for the crime she had committed.

She fervently wished that her daughter had survived and that life would allow them to meet so she could ask her for forgiveness, before facing the court of God.

One day, after confessing to her spiritual guide, Father Stefanio, she decided to tell her father everything, ask his forgiveness and ask for his help to discover her daughter's whereabouts.

Deeply depressed by the immense sadness of seeing her lose her beauty and vitality, aware that death would soon lead her "to the world of shadows", he forgave her and promised to do everything possible to take care of her.

From then on, he began a search that had proved to be very difficult.

※※※

The next day, after so many emotions and a bad night's sleep, Panderva awoke to a great movement in the house, a roar of voices and wailing...

Her heart began to beat fast. She understood quickly. Her mother had detached herself from her body to enter into the plane of the invisible and to travel there the paths that correspond to her as to any other person, when the time comes.

During the night, under extreme medication that did not do her any good, Carlota gave her soul to God, in peace because her daughter had returned to her family and had forgiven her.

In the midst of her agony, her confessor gave her the "holy viaticum", while her father held her hand in tears, calling her name and begging her not to leave...

Fernando feels a lot of pain. His heart; however, reminds him that another sweetheart has arrived who will bring him great comfort and companionship.

Finally, life goes on and new purposes will be brought with it, after all, you will not be alone...!

After the funeral, deeply saddened by not having met her mother sooner, Panderva asks her grandfather for some time to decide what she really wants for her life.

Her grandfather understands and gives her total freedom so that she, overwhelmed by so much information and probable changes, can reflect on her future.

He will legally recognize her as soon as he can. Panderva returns to Wladimir's house.

There, together with Forbes and Cyrene, and mainly under Wladimir's guidance, she reflects on her next steps.

This house has been your blessed beacon, a haven of peace and security, a respectful and joyful coexistence. How could she leave and assume the unknown of another reality? She does not feel ready for that, after all, she has recently changed and accepted the safety of the Vladosk house.

Cuddling her little dog, she spends endless hours in silence in the courtyard of the house, reflecting.

A few days later, with Felizardo prancing at her side, she headed "home." She wanted to go over everything, to feel again what that past had represented in her life.

She wandered, carefree for hours, observing here and there, watching people and remembering situations she had experienced so many times.

She never saw Minerva again. Perhaps she is looking for her elsewhere.

What she does not know, however, is that after receiving a considerable sum of money from Wladimir, Minerva left, happy and hopeful, in search of her lover who resides in a distant place.

With her new economic resources, she was better received.

What she did know was that, like Carlota, she would soon be held accountable for her actions in Heaven.

Both had commitments linked to Panderva's existence, but they failed miserably.

Wladimir, Norbert, Cyrene and Forbes are part of another group of good souls who have known her for a long time; they committed themselves to her spiritual transformation and today do everything possible to support her in her new actions, this time aimed at genuine good and true love.

¡La vita é così...!

A couple of days later Panderva tells Wladimir that she has decided to live with her grandfather:

– Kind man, dear friend, I don't have enough or adequate words to thank you for all you have done for me! God allowed me to meet you in the desert that was my life and you have become for me a desired and beneficent oasis! With you I always found the help I needed, respect and consideration; here my hopes of having a home and the legal recognition of myself were born!

Despite this decision of mine, which is not irrevocable, I intend to do my best to get used to the house that should have been my home from the beginning.

I will finally realize my dreams of having a family. However, I request your consent to return here at any time and make use of your hospitality.

Excited, Wladimir replies:

– My dear friend, the doors of our house and the doors of our hearts will always be open for you! I hope you won't forget us! Be very happy in your new life!

Unable to answer, she nods, trying not to cry...

– Please tell your grandfather to look for me at the Provincial Court, I want to talk to him!

Panderva leaves, and watching her walk away, Wladimir reflects on the near future. Visualizing radical changes in his and his son's life...

The solution for Panderva's life arrives just in time. With her grandfather, she will have protection and love. For him and his household, she will bring wisdom, affection for her fellow man and admirable example of strength and moral courage.

– "Anyway, everyone will win...!" – Wladimir concludes.

Fernando appears at the Provincial Court and is received by Wladimir:

– Welcome! Sit down and make yourself comfortable!

– Thank you, dear sir! I am very grateful, I must express my gratitude for everything you have done for my dear granddaughter, I know that in your home she found everything she needed and what life denied her due to circumstances we both know!

Too moved, Fernando takes a break that Wladimir takes advantage of:

– Mr. Fernando, I also want to mourn the great loss of your daughter Carlota! May her soul be healed and have found mercy with God!

– May it be so...!

– I asked you to come for the final signatures of the papers that legalize, according to your will and that of the interested party, the indissoluble family bond that from now on is officially recognized and legally enshrined in the name of law.

Let me tell you with great emotion that she chose her new civil name in honor of my wife, Isolde, long deceased and mother of my son Norbert, whom she only knew through our nostalgia. Her granddaughter also stated that she chose this name to feel part of our family, I assure you, my dear sir, that she honors us and makes us happy with this strong declaration of affection!

– Anyway, we have much to thank life itself for!

– Certainly, dear Count!

Fernando answers with conviction:

– Me, I have more to be thankful for because I don't even deserve this!

– If so, things would not have ended as they did. The Creator always has great plans for all of us.

Sighing, Fernando hesitates:

– If you say so...

Wladimir adds:

– From this day on, dear Count, you are directly responsible for the fate of this girl who today finds herself astonished by a new reality. She will need a lot of understanding. I hope you will get along very well! I want to reaffirm that she will always have a reserved place in my house and the affection of all of us!

– Thank you, once again and always!

After talking for a long time, they shake hands and say goodbye.

Wladimir sighs in relief. It seems to him that Panderva's old problems finally have a solution.

He quickly recalls his and his son's situation, given the uncertainties of the future...

Their enemies, at the moment, are enjoying their new successes, occupied by their demanding personalities that need constant attention.

So, for the time being, they cannot proceed with their plans.

Father and son intensify arrangements to live outside of Florence. Reason tells them that this is the most logical solution.

22.– THE ENGAGEMENT

In the lighted salons, the baron and his daughter receive their guests.

The commotion of the conversations and the different attractions are harmonized with the music performed by virtuosos, who playing the most varied instruments, are dispersed in different spaces, decorated with the intention to dazzle and entertain, without hiding the obvious intention of simultaneously exhibiting the regal power of the family coats of arms.

Almost always there are parties for celebrations, tributes and to forget the daily stresses that everyone faces indiscriminately.

A great majority likes any kind of fun, without responsibility and without limits. Those unfortunate of soul seek to suffocate the heart's cry with the intense and deceptive noises of crowds and celebrations.

For Brunilda, the ephemeris resembles a sentence, because, despite her will, her destiny is decided by her father, aiming only at his interests.

As the festivities unfold, noisy, attractive and crowded, she shudders with fear of what is surely to come. Inwardly, she has already decided that under no circumstances will she submit to the will of her father or anyone else, for she will never give up the happiness she longs to live with Norbert, her one true love. She will die for it, if necessary, because living according to the will of others was never part of her nature.

Her father, as always, underestimates her ability to react and fight for what she wants.

That's why she receives so many blows.

Von Braun forgets that he and his daughter are made of the same mold; he imposes the strength he possesses, and she uses similar strength to defend herself and live as she pleases.

Unfortunately, although they are father and daughter, they fight on opposite sides...

"I will go to Walhalla if necessary; however, fighting for myself and my love...!" – She shouts inwardly.

Whatever comes, it will certainly be better than what she plans for her future.

Since she was a little girl, she learned to articulate and measure the distance between what she wanted and what she could achieve. Thus, she has created countless difficulties for her father, in what life demands of her to defend herself and what she believes in.

She does not plan to carry out anything on this abominable night, but will wait for a more propitious occasion, as the good strategist she is.

And, as expected, during the course of the celebration, she found herself involved in an engagement contract with a nobleman of German descent, powerful, wealthy, haughty, arrogant and as ambitious as her father.

From the first moment she abhorred his presence. That man of arrogant gestures, conceited and hoarse voice, vulgar expressions, strove to win over "his bride."

However, despite Brunilda's rejection and visible displeasure, this baron despised all the others, letting it be known that he was the favorite.

Thus, as if she were in a terrible nightmare, besides sadly enduring the abominable insistence of the one who considered himself her fiancé, Brunilda began to hear, between giggles and indiscreet glances, the comments of her presumed engagement. From that night on, Florence would know that she was the future wife of that nobleman, with her father's approval.

She felt suffocated and dizzy...

Sometimes she wanted to scream in his face that she would never marry him, but the look on her father's face left no doubt about his probable reaction.

With no other way out, she danced with him all night, enduring his rants.

Pressing her insolently against his numerous medals, and though she had pushed him vehemently, he whispered gallant words in her ear and made fabulous promises, amidst studied romantic expressions to say the least...!

– "Poor miserable! – Brunilda concluded – If he knew the enormous distance that separates him from Norbert, in every way, he would flee far away and hide in a very deep hole...! How could someone compare a shining star to this decorated and colorful puppet who believes himself to be a God!"

Noticing her slight smile, the baron said:

– Finally, your soul blooms!

– If I had the gift of seeing souls, I wouldn't even dare to look at most of those in this room! I must confess that I shudder in terror at such a possibility!

Somewhat annoyed, he noted that she had no intention of apologizing for such an abominable perspective.

Resentful, he thinks of the unusual pleasure he will have in "domesticating" such a beautiful and intelligent woman:

– "Winning your heart will be an incomparable pleasure!" – He concludes in vain, while stroking his long, curved mustache.

Very annoyed and exhausted by so much insistence, Brunilda gets rid of him, claiming that she needs to freshen up.

She drags Lucy out of the corridor and they go to the garden.

There she vents her frustration:

– Oh, my friend, what a torment to bear the presence of that puppet! I feel the need to throw my displeasure in his face, but I must be cautious. My father has looked at me many times, reproaching me and somehow warning me of the consequences of my blatant rejection towards this insufferable man!

– Caution is the right word, my friend! Your father has already chosen the baron as his son-in-law!

Realizing this, she shudders as her friend continues talking:

– You, more than anyone, know what he is capable of! I have seen so much; I shudder to think of it! How many times have we cried together, healing the wounds he caused you? I have already lost count!

– You know what I live... My father and many others, cruelly punish their daughters. Sometimes they even take much more extreme measures! I realize that my life and Norbert's are worth nothing against my father's will. The least serious threat is that I go to a convent, because I know that in a moment of rage, he could seriously hurt me and even kill me!

– Poor Brunilda! I do not see a solution for you...

– Neither do I, but I will not submit, no matter what! You will see, Lucy!

– I know you will confront him, my friend. If not now, when you think it is convenient! And how will it be...? I shudder at the thought!

Without even listening to her friend, Brunilda decides:

– I need to talk to Norbert as soon as possible! My sad fate! To be the daughter of such a cruel man...!

Hugging her by the shoulders, Lucy advises:

– Come on, let us go back to the salon. Your father is coming. He will certainly come looking for you, and if you do not go, he will force you to go anyway. Against him you have no defenses.

Taking a deep breath, Brunilda accepts the suggestion and returns to the salon, passing by her father who gives her a terrible look.

Finally, when the unfortunate banquet was over, her father announced and consecrated his daughter's engagement, officially revealing the fact. The celebrations began there and then and the libations began at dawn. Greetings from the guests were not long in coming.

As in a nightmare, Brunilda found herself surrounded by dazzled and insensitive ladies who asked her the most absurd questions she could imagine. Also, amidst laughter that was not respectful, these ladies said things as abominable as their own thoughts and anticipated the intimacies of the future couple.

At times she lost the condition to tolerate them, answering them with bitterness.

However, those who had surrounded her for exhausting hours understood something, after all, the baron was radiant and, consequently, they should be radiant too. They attributed the bride's bad mood to the excessive pampering the father must give her.

Some rolled their eyes and sighed looking at the "groom", wishing they were in Brunilda's place.

23.– THE OCCASION

Aware of the urgency of making decisions, Brunilda decides to ask Mina for a favor in such a way that she cannot refuse:

– Mina, for heaven's sake! Help me to rest my poor head after what I went through during the party! I need fresh air and rest, please!

– Where do you want to "rest", Brunilda? Aren't you joking as you always do?

– Me, joking with you, my dear Mina? I would not be able to! But if you really love me, you will help me, won't you?

With Brunilda's gentle eyes on her, Mina wanted to know:

– With whom will you go?

– I will invite Lucy and we will have Percival's competent surveillance! Have you forgotten him?

– No... How to forget such a beautiful man, right? – She giggles and hides her face.

– That's right! Besides being handsome, he is very careful!

– Hum... I will do it too! That way your father will trust more!

– Do it, Mina!

All arranged, the next day very early, everyone gets ready for the ride.

Mina arranges everything, but Brunilda, attentive, waits until she is alone in the room, then goes out and locks the door from the outside.

Her father is not at home and the other servants are busy in other spaces away from her room. Then, after many breathless cries, the tired mistress falls asleep and comes to the conclusion that her protégée is in fact a little imp. She hopes that she will return as soon as possible, especially before the baron returns home.

Hours later, parking the carriage on a slope, Percival sees Norbert at a reasonable distance, waiting for them. Lucy had notified him in advance of the time and place where they were to meet.

Brunilda walks down the slope with Lucy.

Carefully, she scans everything around her and heads towards him.

Lucy discreetly walks away and leaves them alone.

Huddled quietly, they both show extreme physical dejection.

Norbert did not sleep. He knew of the event and feared it.

Brunilda did not even go to bed. After the party, seeing her fate decided, she gave herself up to tears and this partially relieved her heart.

Lucy decides to talk to Percival and goes back up the hill. Somewhere hidden among some bushes, Brunilda and Norbert are talking:

– Here we are, my love, and my pain. I know everything... It was clear as day that this would happen!

Huddled in Norbert's heart, she replies:

– I am willing to take any action that can free us from this bond that is binding my life without my consent! As you know, my father is powerful and there is no doubt that there will be repercussions!

Looking at her, firm and affectionate, Norbert makes the hypothesis:

– How would you feel about leaving Florence forever? Would you leave everything behind for us?

Holding his gaze with the same affection, she asks him in a bitter tone:

– What would I be leaving behind, Norbert? Wealth, luxury, power, an empty artificial life? The slavery I have always suffered because of a mercenary father, a stifling reality and a somber future?

Compassionate, Norbert deeply regrets the life of the woman who represents everything to him.

Expanding her thoughts, Brunilda bravely says:

– Even if everything were different and I had to bet on indisputable values, I would act the same way. My life belongs only to me and my Creator! If He Himself grants us complete freedom, it must be so! What is life worth if you are not by my side? We are inseparable!

It is decided! I will do whatever you want! I know without a doubt that what you determine will be the sacred echo of my own will! Tell me when, where and how, and I will follow you without looking back!

Holding her tightly and passionately, completely submitted to the charms of this woman who is the reason for his existence, he whispers:

– My invincible warrior...! I love you...!

– We are the same, my beloved, and I love you too...!

In the meantime, two sour-faced men appear slyly. With a look of birds of prey, they observe everything around them. They descend cautiously from another angle, like predators sniffing for prey.

The two men saw Lucy and Percival, but they did not notice their presence.

Norbert; however, who from a very young age was always committed to defending himself and his father, saw them immediately. He asks Brunilda to keep quiet and they hide under a larger shadow, which allows them to observe the men, waiting for their next actions.

One of them, having noticed Percival and Lucy's loneliness, approaches while the other, patting the pistol at his waist, watches.

Putting himself on guard, Percival takes up a defensive position. He covers the girl and waits.

Lucy shudders and feels paralyzed.

– Oh, good man! – exclaims the one who arrives mischievously –. Are you planning to run away? – As he speaks, he approaches, scrutinizing everything around him.

– What do you take me for? This vehicle belongs to Baron Odorico, as you can easily see from the coat of arms!

Without slowing his pace making Lucy's heart pound, he approaches the vehicle and "sniffs" like a hunting dog, analyzing every corner and finally noticing that it is completely empty.

His companion does not miss a single gesture of the three of them and Norbert does the same, ignored and from a distance.

Aware that the carriage is empty, he asks curiously:

– And what are they doing in such a deserted place? Or would it be better if I do not ask? – He winks in malicious complicity.

– Even if it does not concern you, we stopped to rest!

– Ah! So, you are going somewhere? Hum... I know... May I know where? Maybe it is also useful for us, as a timely trip!

Percival refuses to answer and the other says:

– Well, see you later! Beware of bandits! – At the allusion, mocking and appropriate for the occasion and for his "profession", he bursts out laughing.

Percival maintains his defensive position, while the two walk away exchanging glances.

Lucy breathes and does not even imagine where and how Norbert and Brunilda will be.

Seeing that everything has been resolved, Norbert quickly and silently drags Brunilda into the virgin forest that surrounds the entire region.

The place is perfect for strategic escapes and offers great hiding possibilities.

Thus, after a vertiginous run, they approach a cave, in which the vegetation disguises the entrance nicely. Walking carefully and going as far as possible, they hide. Groping in the gloom, Norbert finds a larger space that seems appropriate. There, silent and expectant, they remain comfortable.

Brunilda heroically controls her fear of running into a snake or other crawling animal.

After a time that seemed interminable to them, they hear footsteps and two voices, arguing about the right path. Between blasphemies, they blame each other.

After a long search, tired and discouraged, they sit down and engage in conversation:

– The coachman and his friend are upstairs, but where are the baron's daughter and Finorio? It is very deserted here and you are very stupid! Who told you they would be here?

– This was the indication I received!

– Those two up there look very comfortable...! We have searched the surrounding area meter by meter and nothing...!

– We could return!

– Return, idiot? Have you forgotten that we have the task of returning only with the one we are looking for, dead or alive?! Would you dare to return and say that we could not do our job?!

– Of course not... But if we do not return, we will not get paid!

– Paid for what, you rascal? If we have nothing, why would we demand the reward?

– Oh... God is not fair to me! – The other whines like a disconsolate child.

The other thinks, stands up and declares emphatically:

– Very well! What is done is done! And what has not been done will throw us into an eternal hole if we do not escape quickly!

Trembling, the other stares at his companion, as he makes a decision:

– From now on, it is every man for himself! Do what you want, because I already know where I am going! Goodbye...!

He looks at his companion and says:

– Anyway, I am getting rid of you, you idiot! I never want to see you again!

Then he leaves, hurriedly and without looking back. Percival and Lucy, distressed, are worried about the couple's delay.

Out of prudence, Norbert and Brunilda remain hidden. They do not know what they will find when they leave. Trembling, she thought that at any moment some reptile would pass by her and climb on her clothes.

The despised man does not know where to go, but still he escapes, aimlessly and without destination.

The hours feel like an eternity.

Percival and Lucy decide to look for Norbert and Brunilda, which they do in vain.

The afternoon is over and the night is not long.

Terrified, they decide to return. What will they say? Any explanation will be useless!

The baron's cruelty is widely known and if it is about the disappearance of his daughter, it would be impossible to guess his reactions.

– Percival, if we return, they will kill us! – Lucy commented in tears. She never imagined herself in a similar situation. The purpose was a simple walk...

– Like us, Norbert must also have seen those men. Surely he knew they were at risk.

– And what would they have done?

– They certainly ran away...! This guy must know the surroundings very well!

– And what will we do?

– We will do the same! We have no other way out...!

Rubbing her hands together in despair, Lucy feels like she is in a nightmare.

Percival thinks, thinks... Little by little, he remembers that he has a small and distant house where some relatives still live.

Whenever he can, he goes to see them.

For the moment it is the best solution. He invites Lucy and she accepts. He waits for the girl to get comfortable inside and urges the horses to run wild. In just a few hours, they leave the confines of Florentine city life.

In the nearby village and in an uninhabited place, he hides the emblazoned carriage to board another, simple and without ornaments. In case they find the carriage, they will have already left.

Lucy is still crying. She is leaving her life behind... Her family will search for her, in vain. They will think she is dead somewhere... She regrets leaving without explaining the situation or saying goodbye to them... How could she have known this would happen to her?!

Now she regrets getting involved, but it's too late for regrets.

Percival looks after her like a beloved daughter and so they travel for many days, trying to stay alive.

"The future is God's and he knows what he is doing...!" – Percival concludes, saddened by the new reality they must live.

The green fields emerge lush, showing a great variety of plantations, most of them vineyards.

In the evening, Norbert and Brunilda leave the cave.

If it were not for the silvery moon, the darkness would be complete.

Returning the way he came, Norbert carefully rescues his horse. Fortunately, he had left it well hidden.

He mounts it and encourages the animal, which quickly starts to run... There is no turning back...

After many hours of riding, he rents a carriage.

– What we planned, my dear, fate has precipitated it!

– Divine wisdom reaches us everywhere in this Universe! Leaving everything behind eases my heart, but as for you...

– It is true, I do not feel comfortable because of my father; however, for the moment, we have no other alternative, but this one. He will surely sense that we are making this decision by force of circumstance... As soon as I can, I will let him know.
I will find out how to do it without putting him or us at risk.

Determined and courageous, both flee, creating the greatest possible distance between them and their enemies, and taking different paths to get lost.

Little by little they walk away from their beloved Florence.

That same night, Wladimir, sleepless, suffers the uncertainty of his son's fate.

If someone comes looking for him, he will say that Norbert is on a business trip and he will keep that version as long as necessary. Unsure, with the weight of doubt, he goes to the oratory, kneels down and prays fervently:

"Father and Creator of us all! Only the Lord alone can see the anguish of my heart! Where will my son be? Will I receive news about him? I have a feeling that some more serious and urgent circumstance has taken him away! What I ask, in the name of your Son, is that, wherever he may be, he may count on your protection...! Knowing that will give me strength and hope...!"

Feeling calmer, he tries to rest a little. The dawn is breaking and he feels a great lassitude.

God will take care of Norbert and Brunilda. His heart feels that the two are together.

– "Norbert will communicate, as soon as he can..." – He concludes.

That night the coachman Percival, Baron Odorico's daughter and her friend Lucy disappeared from Florence.

Despite having searched in every possible and imaginable place, the baron could not discover where his "treasure" was. He was also surprised by the absence of Percival and Lucy, who also could not be found to give their statements. After all, they were together! He suspects a deliberate escape and at this thought he becomes furious. In the midst of uncontrolled and violent attitudes, he makes threatening inquiries and distributes different orders in all directions.

He sent a courier to Lucy's residence to conduct an investigation. Concerned, he himself inspected Percival's room in the servants' quarters, waking everyone up. Even the pets reacted, each in their own way.

In patent desperation, Lucy's parents, angry and offended, threatened the baron and his house, accusing him of the disappearance of their beloved daughter.

Brunilda and Lucy, inseparable friends, often stay together for several days and weeks, on trips, outings and entertainments, which is consented by the two families of equal power and prominence.

A few days later, rumors spread around town about the disappearance of the baron's daughter and her friend, causing even more confusion.

Wladimir maintains the statement that his son is far away, due to his profession and business.

Although he doubts it, the baron has no evidence to the contrary. Completely disoriented, he ponders, ponders, and no matter how much he ponders, he cannot even come up with an idea to begin a more fruitful search.

– "The ones I hired to follow Brunilda have disappeared too...! Is there some spell in this?" – He shudders at the thought.

He sent competent professionals in all directions to investigate the case.

Brunilda's future fiancé saddened and disgusted, declares to the four winds that he has fallen in love with the beautiful future consort and he is not resigned to lose her – and certainly she increases the prestige and financial power he already wields in Florence, and in his Germania.

24.- THE POWER OF THE PAST

Countess Isolde de Alencar Nogueira, formerly Panderva, whom from now on we will call by her official name, made herself comfortable living in her grandfather's house, since, once there, she was surprised by the welcome and affection of everyone.

If she were still living with Minerva, she could never have guessed that life still had so much to offer her.

Prudence, her mother's maid, embraced her tightly. In her loving heart, the daughter took the place of the mother, who had always been "her child."

Isolde is intimately grateful to God and the good man.

She often visits Wladimir's house and, whenever possible, has excellent conversations with her dear friend.

She also talks with Cyrene and Forbes, who very special to her heart. In addition, she has been keeping a close eye on Forbes' health and has already invited her to live in "her home."

Her grandfather makes her comfortable and gives her constant pampering and attention.

With this "new opportunity," Fernando is trying to appease the soul of his beloved daughter Carlota.

Winning everyone's heart with her spontaneous way of being and her kindness, Isolde does not neglect to watch over her own feelings and inclinations, for in spite of the hard lesson life has given her, as it happens to many others, she still has her old ways.

She was so devoted to her new life that she would make anyone believe she had been born and lived there forever. She is very comfortable in a rich and comfortable environment.

This was her "Achilles' heel...!"

She often goes out with Prudence to go shopping and walk around beautiful Florence, now with a new perspective and hope for life.

In a fashion store, where she is choosing a beautiful hat, she is surprised by Theobald's presence.

The latter, seeing her through the window, very anxious, enters and approaches her, without her noticing.

–Excuse me...!

Turning around, she almost loses her breath.

– Yes? – She answers, hiding her shock and insecurity.

– Do you remember me?

She could tell him no and he would not dare to contradict her, since he is a gentleman... But how could she do such a thing when deep in her heart she shudders with pleasure at the mere tone of his voice?

– And then? – He insists excessively anxious with his eyes shining.

– Where and when? – She asks.

– The day I saw you hugging your little dog and crying, sympathizing with the pain of those who die cruelly, penalized by the law of the Church, do you remember? Do not say no, I beg you! This would be too frustrating for me, who have been looking for you for so long!

– Were you looking for me? Why? – She defies him haughtily, as if this reunion did not matter to her at all.

– Because I could not forget you!

He uses a seductive voice that Isolde ignores in this life.

– And did you try to do it? – She insists deliberately.

– Why would I do that if I wanted to see you again? Anyway, here we are!

Analyzing him, from top to bottom, with an appearance of indifference, Isolde asks:

– Are you always so imprudent?

Laughing and bending down to get closer, Theobald answers:

– Not always! Only when something interests me too much, like now!

– Ah...! And do you have the habit of approaching a girl in such a careless way?

Giving her an increasingly ardent look, he lowers his voice and whispers seductively:

– No. Usually, I am very discreet but in front of you, it is impossible to control myself! You cannot imagine how much I have dreamed of this moment...

Prudence, who is listening to everything, sometimes stands between the two of them, with an angry and inquisitive face.

The young woman sometimes laughs at the amusing situation.

He, more and more enchanted, prays:

– Please do not say you forgot me...! And do not judge me hastily! I beg your consent to meet her more often!

In silence, Isolde reflects:

– "If you only knew who we are and the risk we run! I need to run away from you and everything you represent...!"

Faced with her silence, he insists:

– Then what do you say? On your lips are my happiness or my misfortune! Give me a chance, I beg you!

Prudence pulls her lace sleeve and whispers in her ear:

– Beware, my child! This rogue is only trying to get one more! Just that! Do not let yourself be deceived...!

Isolde silently and intentionally ignores him, takes the hat in her hands and, talking to the saleswoman, completes the purchase.

All done, she heads for the exit followed by Prudence. Theobald chases after her, very anxious:

– Do not go, first at least tell me your name and where you live, for all that you love most!

The words "where you live" made her think that if he had known who she was and where she lived when they met, this reunion would never take place, because he would have revealed, without shame, his contempt, if not in words, by acts...

Standing there, with the box in her hands and Prudence pulling her by the arm, preventing her from thinking clearly, Isolde feels that her reason and her heart suggest completely opposite solutions.

Gently, she releases herself from Prudence, pushing her away. She takes a deep breath, turns to Theobald and looks at him silently.

There is great anxiety in his eyes and he is moved. In an emotion as great as his, she shudders. The gaze of that man penetrates effortlessly into his captive and faithful soul with a feeling that travels through time...

He insists, more and more anxious:

– And so, are you going to leave me like this, without telling me who you are and where you live?

Submitting to the voice of her heart, Isolde answers:

– My name is Isolde and if you want to see me again as you say, I will be back in this store a week from now!

She cannot help thinking:

– "Some time ago, I would not have dared even to tell you my name...!"

He bends down, fixes his cat pupils in her eyes and kisses her hand:

– I will be here waiting for you! These will be the longest days of my life!

Isolde rushes out, dragging Prudence with her. She felt that her heart would burst out of her mouth and she could still visualize that ardent eyes on her.

Prudence understood everything: her girl, despite the bluffs, is as interested as he is.

She hated the boy's presence. She found it rude and invasive. Isolde is anxious about the next encounter. Maybe it's better that she does not go...

A week has passed, she thinks... She sighs and concludes that in front of this man she has no defenses, nor does she want to have any. She needs him like the air she breathes. The strong feeling that once united them is still powerful, for her luck or her ruin.

"Can I escape this fate? The more appropriate question would be: Do I want to escape this fate... No! Everything in me leads me towards it, again and again! Oh, foolish heart! What will come? I trust only in God, for I will listen to no one else...!"

When she gets home, she listens patiently and with some indifference to Prudence's affectionate admonitions, while imagining her reaction when she finds out that Forbes will soon be coming to live there. She had already asked the kind man, who without words, showed his excitement and approval.

25.– THE LETTER

A few days passed.

One afternoon, when activities were intense at the Provincial Court, Wladimir received a visit from someone asking for privacy. Such a procedure is common and almost always justified by the person's desire to be safe, but his heart could not help but jump out of his chest.

The night before he had dreamed about Norbert. It was such a real dream that he woke up talking to him, as they used to do, so fraternal...

Upon receiving the person in question, he gives orders not to be interrupted under any circumstances.

On entering his office, the man greets him elegantly and politely:

– My respects, Mr. Wladimir Vladosk! I have the task of delivering an important missive for you. Here it is!

Reading the sender's name, Wladimir confirms his intuition: the letter is from Norbert!

He opens it and reads it, anxiously:

"Dear Mr. Wladimir Vladosk!

Respectful greetings!

Confirming my appreciation and admiration for you, I inform you that our business is on track to achieve great results. I inform you that for business reasons, we will have to make an urgent and long trip to ensure the success of our company! I am waiting for you with great urgency!

Sincerely yours!

Grateful and reverent,

Ivo de Santorini"

"Dear son! – he thinks with emotion –. Definitely...!"

However, concealing the joy that overcomes him, he thanks and rewards the courier with a handsome recompense. He knows that his son must have done it already, but that man will never have an exact idea of the great favor he is doing him at that blessed moment. In his heart he will henceforth call him a divine courier.

He smiles at the thought.

The courier makes his way to the exit, between bows of thanks. Alone, Wladimir rereads each line of the letter, filled with emotion and longing.

He then burns the missive and organizes his thoughts, before taking the next steps:

"Today I will take the necessary steps to do what I must, as soon as possible. I have already thought of those I care most about, such as Cyrene and Forbes... To both of them I owe a lot over all these years and it is necessary to keep them safe and sound.

Cyrene, friend and companion in so many struggles! I will finance your return to your land by compensating you royally. He has long declared that when old age comes – despite his stubbornness to ignore that he already has his life settled –, he intends to return to Genoa and spend the rest of his days near the grave of his beloved and unforgettable daughter.

My dearest Forbes, angel of my home, aged and tired... She certainly wants, though she does not say so, to be with Isolde, to whom she has grown too fond. My dearest Forbes, angel of my home, aged and tired... She certainly wants, though she does not say so, to be with Isolde, to whom she has become too fond. Isolde's wish, therefore, will be fulfilled sooner than we imagine. I will give Forbes some good savings. I have no doubt that she will be very well by the side of her naughty girl, because Isolde will look after her with great affection.

Forbes and Cyrene contributed a lot to make sure that we were always well and comfortable in our home. Services and dedication like this are worth gold...! Facing day to day life with peace of mind, in terms of managing our home, has always made a difference in my life and my son's life... May heaven bless and reward you!"

Looking around, he concludes that this stage of her life is coming to an end. The future will be a great unknown.

Taking a deep breath, he finishes:

– ¡*Alea jacta est*...! World! Here I go! And may the heavens be favorable to us! We will navigate by the divine compass of the Creator with love, hope and great faith!

He reflects on what to do:

"My departure from Florence has to be strategic and mysterious... I need to move fast... Very soon, I hope to be embracing my dear son! Oh Lord, how much I have to thank you...!"

On this day, Wladimir leaves work early.

For long minutes he observed, grateful and affectionate, every piece of furniture, work equipment and the ambient decoration that always brought him comfort and convenience to work...

As he left, he embraced his employees with emotion. He would probably never see them again...

He did all this in a playful and discreet way. No one can suspect that he will never return to the Provincial Court of the beautiful and flourishing Italian city that dominated the dreams of his youth, filling him with plans, almost all accomplished... He will continue to love and venerate it wherever he goes. Much of his and his son's history will be there forever.

On the way back, he admires every space so familiar for the last time... as well as so many other things, which will now be part of the past.

As the carriage sways, he ends up dozing.

When he arrives, he calls Cyrene.

– How did you guess, Mr. Wladimir, that the letter was from Norbert?

– My good friend Ivo de Santorini already gave his soul to God some time ago. Only Norbert and I know that. In this letter, my son tells me everything I need to know and even if it fell into the wrong hands, it would not represent any danger.

– Excellent!

– Cyrene, I must travel as fast as I can and I have no intention of returning.

Cyrene is surprised. Agitated, he asks pertinent questions and Wladimir explains his intentions for his near future:

– I advise you to get out of here fast. If they come looking for me, you will be in danger, my friend. God protect you always! My son and I are grateful to you for everything, Cyrene!

With his head down, tears falling, Cyrene understands. He knows that what is at stake is very serious and it is better not to get involved.

– Life has decided so and God will take care of all of us, Mr. Wladimir! – He exclaims in tears.

Enraptured, he embraces Wladimir, who with tears in his eyes, returns the gesture of friendship.

– Tell Forbes to come talk to me and then get ready to take her to Isolde's house!

– Yes, sir!

Cyrene leaves and in a few minutes Forbes enters Wladimir's office:

– Are you looking for me, kind man?

– Yes!

Curious, sits in front of him.

– "Cyrene was moved and saddened, what will Forbes' reaction be like?" – He thinks.

– Forbes, dear friend! Some recent events force me to travel far away!

– Oh...! You are leaving Florence?

– Yes, but no one must know! This is for me and Norbert's safety!

– Where is he?

– Away from here. It was necessary.

– We did not even say goodbye! – She comments sadly.

– I could not even do it. Circumstances caused that unexpected decision.

– It's okay.

– Yes! Praise the Lord!

–Amen…!

– Before I go, I want you to be safe! That is why I am asking you to go to Isolde. I know this is what you both want.

– It is true! I miss her so much...!

– Things were rushed, Forbes, and what would be done in a timely and calm manner must be done quickly for the safety of all.

– I will do as you command, Mr. Wladimir. After all, even when you are in trouble, you protect us and somehow help us! May God reward you for such kindness and wisdom!

– My dear Forbes, thank life itself for the appreciation you have given me so much over the years! You will receive your payment plus securities so that you can subsist for a long time and with peace of mind. Thank you for everything and I will never forget you!

Already in tears, Forbes bows slightly and leaves. His heart, which already has so much experience in life, tells her she will never see him again.

The thought of being with Isolde partly comforts her. Leaving her at Count Fernando's mansion and with Isolde, to whom he explained in a few words that Wladimir and his son were going on a business trip, but that she was not to tell anyone, Cyrene said goodbye to the young woman.

On his return, he found his boss in the midst of the hustle and bustle of packing suitcases and luggage.

– Cyrene, I still need a favor!

– At your service, sir!

– We are the same height and weight, aren't we?

– Yes!

– Lend me one of your simpler clothes and a hat too.

– I will do it right now!

Cyrene gives him his clothes, thinking:

– "The boss knows what he is doing!"

Wladimir, who for some time had been discharging papers and documents and any financial dependencies and who had also moved his business to another city as a precaution, put an end to it all.

He emptied the drawers of papers and manuscripts related to his scientific studies and packed everything up to take with him.

He provided Cyrene with enough money for his old age, wherever he went.

He was alone, meditating...

He walked around the house, saying goodbye to it and all that he had lived there...

He cried... How could he not do it? He was about to leave everything behind!

In Norbert's room he organizes what to take with him.

Late at night, dressed in the clothes that belonged to Cyrene and putting on his head the hat that partially covers his face, he leaves the house, gets into a rented car with his suitcases and luggage, and says goodbye forever to his beloved Florence...

– "May the Lord be with me...!" – He thinks and leans back comfortably on the seat, while tears fall on Cyrene's clothes, wetting them...

Admiring himself in the servant's clothes, he concludes:

– "Good friend, Cyrene, Heaven preserve thee, I shall miss thee!"

26.– THE CARDINAL'S DEPARTURE

Some time later, Don Anastacio decides to return to his place, as he calls Rome, where he lives and acts in a powerful and Machiavellian way among his peers.

Dispensing with anyone's approval, he starts a small revolt all around him, with the declared intention of destabilizing everything and everyone once again, while organizing his own retreat.

Amidst the many baggage and regal gifts, he declares that he is eager to travel, but mentions nothing about his next destination. He nourishes with pleasure the mystery that surrounds him.

The same paraphernalia that of his arrival is set up for his departure, leaving those who should be at his disposal in turmoil. The rush and bustle he sees is remarkable, with unbelievable events and surprising movements.

The beautiful city is confused, dazed, out of place, facing each other as enemies or seeing themselves as companions.

In order not to succumb under the same storm, they help each other, although they wish the other would disappear from the face of the planet.

Impatient, shouting and dressed in inappropriate clothes, Mr. Anastacio scolds those who run hither and thither, demanding more efficiency, competence, obedience and, above all, results. It is quite amusing to see the most prominent authorities jumping from one side to the other, attending to your smallest and almost always unreasonable demands.

Mocking everything and everyone, he seems to have simply the function of disrupting the institutions, of which he is a part, to demonstrate his ineffectiveness.

This is how the hours go by, in spectacles at least worthy of the comedies in the variety theaters.

Mr. Anastacio roars and declares to the despair of many that he has already made his report and that he will take it to those who direct the destinies of any city subject to the Church, which conforms immense and even unsuspected territories.

However, almost everyone knows that this man, a religious by profession and not by faith, a "conductor of souls" as he calls himself, declared and assumed superior, has long since declined his own dignity.

However, the heraldry he wears and represents is in fact too official and too serious to be despised.

27.– WISDOM

In her grandfather's house, which is now also hers, Isolde goes on with her life doing the best she can, given what is already established.

The grandfather has become so fond of his granddaughter that he sometimes mistakes her for his beloved daughter, Carlota. On these occasions, to his aching heart, time stood still and nothing that happened really happened...

She understands and knows that as time goes by, he will accept reality more and more.

Her spontaneous joy and kindness win over his heart more and more and he, captivated by her charms, spends hours by her side, listening with interest to her experiences even though she is so young.

The little dog runs and barks all over the house, with everyone's approval.

He is and always will be his owner's best friend, until the day he leaves the world.

Finally, Forbes, with Isolde's appreciation and help, masterfully adopted the habits and customs of the Nogueira household.

However, her rheumatism becomes more and more intense and, consequently, very painful.

The treatments she receives partially alleviate the crises, which lead her to experience periods of great suffering in bed.

✶ ✶ ✶

Like Forbes and Prudence, thousands of other women fulfill, although they have no children, their feminine desires, dedicating themselves to the children of other mothers, on whom they disinterestedly pour the sublime feeling of unconditional love that nature itself bestows on them.

The Creator has relied on these creatures over millennia to substitute the absence of biological mothers, and how many times, throughout our evolutionary journeys, have we benefited from this admirable and precious love? What if we did not come out of their wombs? These women have appreciated us, educated us, loved us, even sacrificed themselves and followed in our footsteps even after the death of the body.

Many times, for unknown reasons, and by the mercy of the Lord for all of us, wonderful mothers of heart crossed our paths...!

Throughout the reincarnations, in the exchange of benefits, we make a healthy and legitimate rotation in the different family attributions and we find ourselves, here and there, as fathers, mothers, children, grandchildren, nephews, nieces, in-laws, forming a beautiful and leafy tree, which will give its shade and protection on account of the love given and received.

I, Rochester, from the bottom of my soul, owe you much and kiss your generous hands.

✶ ✶ ✶

When she feels well, Forbes likes to take care of the garden. With her magic hands, the garden is more beautiful than before.

In that garden, Isolde reads the books she enjoys most, especially those to which she had access in the house of the kind man – paternal friend that life has given her...!

She misses Cyrene too, but this dear friend has left Florence.

– Forbes, and Cyrene? Do you know where he went?

– I can't even imagine, daughter! We said goodbye the day I arrived here! When I said goodbye to my good friend Cyrene, we embraced affectionately and I thanked him for his goodwill, understanding and the time we spent together.

– Dear Cyrene... Who would have thought that your life would change so much?

– Our lives have changed a lot, haven't they?

– Yes! And in spite of everything, we have nothing to complain about. Do you agree?

– I certainly do! I am grateful to heaven and to all those who support me, especially now with this persistent disease!

– There are other diseases, my dear Forbes, and worse! So, do what your doctor tells you, okay?

– And do I have a choice?

– No!

They both laughed.

Forbes leaves and Isolde stays there, admiring the beauty of the blue sky and the beautiful flowers cleverly placed and planned to form beautiful, multicolored arabesques.

Fernando comes over and sits down next to her:

– Hello, my granddaughter! I know you are happy, but I often find you thoughtful, like now.

– Old habit of mine! Do not worry. Those who have had so many experiences cannot ignore the deepest truths of life and this is not always pretty, you know... We, the disinherited, face pain, sadness, violence, disrespect and fear from a very early age.

Fernando lowers his head, sad and ashamed, and she says:

– Please do not feel bad! I have already told you many times that if life has made me go through so much pain it is because for some reason it was necessary!

– How can you say that, my dear? If it were not for my paternal tyranny with Carlota, you wouldn't have lived as you did!

– Grandfather, do not blame yourself. What happened to me had to happen to me!

– Did you learn to overcome life's misfortunes by deceiving yourself?

– No! I learned that, if the Creator is perfect and wise, our lives follow the proper script for our spiritual improvement!

– I do not possess, as you do, my dear, this high understanding. I know I was a source of pain to you and your mother…
I am the one to blame…!

– Calm your heart. God is just, of course, but He is also merciful! Do you know Ecclesiastes?

– Theorically! I was never a man of faith!

– Well, then, Grandpa. There, the psalmist says there is a time for everything…! My purpose was to live as I did, until the moment I met you and my mother! Clearly, the evil I encountered with Minerva was unnecessary and it was all due to her savagery, but what I experienced over the years was part of my spiritual needs.

– You are so young and you reveal so much wisdom…

– I am young, but my soul is very old, dear grandfather. Like anyone else, I face many challenges, given my imperfections.

Reason tells me that I must do the right things, but I do not always succeed.

– Where is the knowledge you reveal based, my child?

– In the divine justice that allows us to be born many times in order to evolve more and more!

– Do you speak of the science of palingenesis?

– Yes! Only then will we be able to understand the differences on earth and the various levels of consciousness of our humanity!

– I never believed in these philosophies coming from the East. I find all this very questionable, but at the same time very opportune! Someone like me who has already made a lot of mistakes, seeks solace and hope in this misunderstood possibility.

– It may be misunderstood, but it is legitimate! The law of reincarnation reflects, powerful and indisputable, the divine justice applied in man, in everything that exists in the Universe and that evolves incessantly under the natural laws.

God, who loves us in a way incomprehensible to our understanding, instead of condemning us, grants us other opportunities to learn, to correct ourselves, encouraging us to an ever more intense spiritual transformation.

That is what we have eternity for, Grandpa!

– So, dear granddaughter, do you think that the two of us knew each other before and that we will be together again...?!

– Yes! Woe to me if I did not believe this unmistakable truth! The certainty of justice and the hope of progress will lead us on a path that will be even better and more successful!

Fernando remains silent.

Isolde takes a deep breath, observes him and comments:

– Now it is you, grandfather, who is thoughtful!

Kissing her on the cheek, neither agreeing nor disagreeing, Fernando gets up and begins to walk away.

She; however, raises her voice and declares:

– What matters, above all, is to learn to be good!

He stops walking, turns around and replies:

– I never learned this!

– What I see today contradicts that statement!

He remains standing, uncertainly listening to her.

– You have repented and you try to correct yourself, even if it is to redeem yourself in front of the dear departed daughter! Tell me, do you believe in God?

Approaching, again, Fernando answers sincerely:

– For a long time I doubted it, but when it brought me back to you, I felt that God exists!

– In spite of everything, God always loves us!

Fernando sits back down and observes that Isolde speaks emphatically, besides being an advocate of the law, when she is in court. His granddaughter is admirable, her cheeks flushed and her eyes bright. There is something greater and incomprehensible about her...

She continues saying:

– "For the transformation of the human heart, there is no magic but a lot of work and inner renovation!

We have old matters to settle, fruit of other existences. As we purify ourselves through our atonements, we gradually improve and prepare ourselves for better and greater futures, where the heart and reason, together and in harmony, will first do the will of the Creator, because our desired happiness will depend in the first instance on the knowledge of His eternal laws!

One day, finally, we will all be happy, but this dreamed happiness will be built, many times, between tears of pain and suffering.

Let no one worry about unimportant things, but think about redemption itself, which will not be done out of selfishness, but through rational, loving and increasingly responsible learning.

Simplicity, prayer, constant solidarity, together with love and the work of intimate transformation, will lead us day after day to true wisdom!

True love must protect and liberate! God created us free to act and to choose paths!

Whoever wants to be good must sincerely strive for it. Transform yourself, "my son", while there is still time and follow your path, until the solemn moment of giving an account to God for your actions, through the judgment of your own conscience. And do not forget to thank heaven for all you have received! Be at peace!"

Fernando cries without understanding the situation. After all, who would have spoken to him? Certainly not his beloved granddaughter.

Isolde falls silent, takes a deep breath, looks around and asks:

– Why are you crying, grandfather? What did I tell you? Forgive me! I haven't told you about my weirdness yet!

– Blessed weirdness, granddaughter! You have taught me a hard lesson. Your mother used to talk like that too! That's the reason why sometimes I used to punish her! I carry the burden of this guilt too!

– Please do not cry... I do not want to be guilty of your pain.

Wrapping his granddaughter in an affectionate embrace, Fernando asks, trying to smile:

– And who said that these tears are of sadness? No! They are of repentance, emotion and joy!

– Ah... I am glad! – She concludes relieved.

Playful and wagging his tail frantically, the little dog makes his owner understand that he needs her company.

Asking permission from her grandfather, she proceeds to give him attention.

The current Countess Isolde, formerly our uncontrollable Panderva, now calls him Felizardo, a name that suits him very well...!

28.– MALICIOUS INTERESTS

The pursuers of Wladimir and Norbert, feeling free to act again, decide to start the scheduled persecutions, but...

When looking for them, they were surprised by their evident absence in Florence.

Amidst the most disparate curses and reactions, they set off for the city, without finding them anywhere. Then, they heard that Norbert had traveled on business and that Wladimir had not appeared at the Provincial Court for a long time.

Rumor has it that father and son have disappeared out of nowhere, as have Baron Odorico's daughter, the coachman Percival and the beautiful Brunilda's friend Lucy.

The people, when talking about it, superstitiously cross themselves, while wondering who will be the next in the mysterious line of missing persons.

Those who planned to destroy them went to their residence and disturbed the neighborhood, without any respect and with violence.

At Wladimir's house; however, the emptiness and obvious abandonment of everything left there made them suspect mysterious events. Nothing to implicate or give them clues as to his whereabouts.

Aristophanes, furious and making use of his unquestioned authority and to the scandal of all present, searched every closet, drawer and corner of the rooms used by the competent lawyers, his personal enemies, chosen from the beginning by his hardened heart.

On leaving, he moved in every direction and, acting in the same manner, amidst the most extravagant exclamations, he loudly demanded that they discover any trace, no matter how small, that might serve as a reference for a possible prosecution of the "two infamous ones."

In high spirits, some tried to set fire to Wladimir's stately estate; however, they were stopped just in time as the beautiful mansion now belonged to the State and the Church.

Finally, no trace of their whereabouts was found, neither documents nor Wladimir's research.

This drove Aristophanes to the brink of madness. In a loud voice, he reproached Greeks and Trojans, as well as swearing revenge.

In a few days, with accounts done and profits negotiated, the new lord seized everything that had cost the former resident a lot of sweat.

Although he snatched almost everything – an intention already consecrated, since before –, dissatisfied, Aristophanes swore in the name of heaven and hell that he would find them and carry out his dreamed revenge!

To do this, he intends to use the accusation of heresy, to which father and son had been publicly subjected some time ago...

Before the Holy Office, at any time or place, their names will be registered in the black list of the Holy Mother Church and they will receive, at any time, what they deserve.

Frustrated, Aristophanes decides to take it out on those who are accused of the same charges.

Isolde wanted to revisit Wladimir's house, but Forbes vehemently prevented her:

– Do not do that! Do not expose yourself! Be worthy of the protection you have been given and take care of your new life! If they suspect you, they will want to torture you to find out where Mr. Wladimir and his son are.

– You are right... The good man would tell me that we should not defy evil...

– Today, no one would recognize you. Officially Panderva never existed! Your new life protects you, as long as you know how to act!

– The best memories of my life are there, my dear Forbes...

– And mine, child...? – She cannot control herself and bursts into disconsolate tears.

The young woman embraces her affectionately and waits for her tears of nostalgia to cease...

The reference to her old name reminds her of the refined women's ornament store and of Theobald. She has not yet decided if she will go to meet him, her soul ardently desires to see him again... In the face of the force of destiny and this ancient affection, she is once again involved in the same feelings, although reason alerts her soul to the suffering this would cause her.

Meanwhile, she thinks wistfully and very worried: "Where are the dear kind man and his son?"

The dog barked loudly and happily. Confident, she put Wladimir and Norbert in God's hands, sending them good wishes, wherever they were...

In the house of Baron Odorico Von Braun, the imbalance is total. There is chaos in the actions and reactions of this arbitrary man, who proclaims to the four winds that he will punish with cruelty refinements those responsible for his daughter's kidnapping.

Brunilda's future fiancé, in turn, expressed his grief; possessed, he proclaimed his hatred and his intentions of revenge. In a loud voice, he promised a large sum to anyone who would bring him reliable clues. Faced with the chaos installed in the baron's house, he took the opportunity to make himself more and more necessary, indefinitely extending his guest status and further strengthening the bonds of friendship and future kinship.

To the "future father-in-law" he promises to find the "beloved bride" and for that he will move heaven and earth.

– And woe to those who cross my way...! – He roars like a madman.

29.– THE RISKS

In Lucy's parents' residence, now immersed in pain and longing, one sleepless night her mother, who is on one of the balconies that allows her to see the surroundings, sees a hidden figure, who from time to time looks up.

Despite the distance, its movements seem familiar. A stronger thought comes to her related to the memory of her daughter. She enters the room and calls her husband.

Trembling, he wakes up and roars:

– What is the matter? Did you see ghosts in the dark of night?

She quickly explains to him what she saw.

– Call the guard! Let me sleep, woman!

– No! Go and see who it is, please!

Although very upset, Harald goes downstairs with one of the guards and heads for the exit.

With a gun in hand, he opens a small door next to the big door and scans the outside.

He runs quickly and catches the person.

Frightened, the masked man does not react and lets his head be uncovered.

Harald very surprised, exclaims:

– Percival! What are you doing here? And what do you want?

– Please calm down, Baron! I come on behalf of your daughter, Lucy!

– Why do you come here like a vulgar thief in the middle of the night?!

– I have already told you! I came to tell you about your daughter!

Moving slowly so that the baron can keep up with him and realize that he has no intention of attacking him, Percival pulls a blue silk handkerchief from his saddlebag and silently displays it.

The baron easily recognizes the object.

With his heart beating madly, the baron sees in that silk handkerchief the foreboding of bad news.

– What does it mean? – He asks extremely anxious.

– It means that I know the whereabouts of your daughter, Baron!

Almost losing his strength, he asks with a weak voice:

– She is alive...!

He begins to shake Percival violently while saying desperately:

– Speak, man!

– Your daughter is alive and well! Please release me before you strangle me!

– That is what I will do if you are lying! This scarf is not enough to believe what you say!

– Please calm down and rest your heart! I will tell you everything, if you let me!

Baron Von Stein partially calms down, releases him and makes a gesture to tranquilize the woman, who struggles from the balcony to understand what they are saying.

Finally, he notices that Percival is drenched in sweat and extremely tired, which means that at any moment he could faint. He invites him upstairs. When they reach the lobby, they stop to attend to Percival's urgent needs.

Thus, while refreshing himself with a little water and greedily eating a piece of bread and roast meat brought to him by the baroness, the baron walks restlessly and angrily.

Between interrupted sentences for chewing, Percival declares:

– It has been days since I ingested enough food. I have been traveling with the intention of finding them. Dear baron and baroness, your daughter is, for her own safety, far away from here. We agreed on something and we need your support and participation.

– Agreed on what? Since when did you and my daughter agree on anything? I would rather have shot you like a dog, useless thing!

Interfering between Percival and her husband, the baroness asks, somewhat impatiently:

– What do you want, man? To spoil the only chance we have of knowing the whereabouts of our daughter? Control yourself! How long have we suffered for not knowing where she is? My heart can no longer bear this uncertainty! For God's sake, for my sake, for Lucy's sake, do what reason determines at this moment! Percival is a good man and has always been worthy of our confidence.

Already accustomed to this, Percival does not expect the baron to apologize or anything similar. He will never submit or give reason to those who are socially inferior to him.

Therefore, he responds politely and carefully:

– Given the circumstances that suddenly involved us, it was necessary to think fast and leave Florence.

– And how did you do it? – asks the baron, with expectant eyes.

– We used the carriage I usually drive and stayed at my family's residence, which is a bit far away.

– In your family's resident?! And where is that?

– In another city, conveniently far from the fury of Baron Odorico and the events that surround us!

As you can see, nothing but the urgency to survive made us decide and act quickly. As we were the only witnesses of Brunilda's disappearance, your daughter, like me, feared the violence of Baron von Braun.

The Baron listens, very intrigued and suspicious:

– To what extent are you involved in Brunilda's disappearance? Were you, and I already fear the answer, accomplices in the flight of your boss's daughter?

– My former boss, if you will excuse me, sir! The answer you are asking for, unfortunately we do not have it and that would involve us dangerously. We are completely unaware of Brunilda's intentions, if she had any. We accompanied her with the intention of assisting her on a walk where she could relax after the shock of her recent engagement.

And Percival goes on to narrate how it all happened, carefully avoiding mentioning Norbert Vladosk. When he finishes, the baron, disgusted, bursts out:

– Who do you think you are? With my power I am able to defend Lucy! I am astonished that she would embark on this grotesque adventure with someone like you! She escapes with a coachman, leaving us here to suffer in the uncertainty of what might have happened to her! How dare she?

In the face of so much aggression, Percival wished he was far away and had never complied with Lucy's request. However, he patiently continued with his explanations:

– Your daughter, very nervous, upon realizing her friend's disappearance, panicked and feared not only for herself, but for you too! That is why she decided to accompany me on the path we took to free ourselves from torture and certain death. My heart broke at the sight of your daughter's utter despair.

Since then, we have been running and hiding. We are currently in a small town. It would be a good idea for you to reflect on the fact that I could have escaped alone, which would have been easier and safer!

At this point, Lucy's mother cries while intimately thanking heaven.

– I believe him, Harald, listen to him and maybe we can see our dear Lucy again!

Percival slaps his forehead and exclaims:

– Ah, I almost forget! – Saying this, he pulls out a thick missive from inside his clothes, in which the girl explains her upcoming plan to her parents, asking for their consent and participation.

– Here is a letter from your daughter!

The baron; however, still has doubts and one of them settles in his heart in a terrible way, within his concepts of nobility and honor. After all, Percival is a strong and physically attractive man, despite his humble condition and this may be, after all, another factor of fascination...

Percival can almost read his thoughts and hopes.

– Where do you fit into all this? – he asks, his hand caressing the gun at his waist.

– I, sir, was in the same place at the same time and became involved in this dramatic situation. I used reason to save both of us while we could. just that! I hope everything works out so I can set my life on a new course. I have plans and I need your daughter to be safe.

Not very convinced, the baron begins to read to his wife the affectionate verses, full of nostalgia that Lucy wrote.

After reading, they wipe away their tears. Finally, the baron suggests:

– Bertha, write to our daughter that we agree to everything!

– I will, Harald, right now!

She leaves and Percival shudders at the thought that this man, as powerful as his former boss, can now eliminate him and get him out of the way. After all, he already knows where Lucy is and can handle situation without his help.

Nevertheless, he waits while husband and wife have a conversation. Then, the baron returns and says:

– Lucy is asking us to trust. For the moment, I will not wait for her to confirm what you said in order to reward you as I should. After all, it seems that we owe you the safety of our dear daughter.

– I need no other reward than what life itself gives me when my conscience approves of my actions. If I had a daughter and she were in a similar situation, I would want someone to do the same!

Von Stein looks at him, believing and doubting.

His heart rejoices, his daughter, whom he assumed dead, is alive and he will soon be able to embrace her.

He decided, together with Bertha, to do everything by mutual agreement and in secret: the social position of both of them and the sadness that invaded the house would allow them to act freely and without suspicions, which in fact has no basis because Lucy is unaware of Brunilda's whereabouts.

Percival hid in the barn of the sumptuous residence of Baron Von Stein and the next day, somewhat recovered, he left discreetly, returning to his place of origin.

When he arrived, he gave Lucy the answer his mother had lovingly written. He also explained to her everything that had happened.

With a renewed soul, the young girl followed Percival's plans and in a few days she was reunited with her parents in another city, far from Florence, to start a new life.

After the happy outcome, Percival traveled through several cities thinking about his own life.

In Genoa, he went to the port to observe the activities of the sailors.

A dreamer, imagining himself as one of them, he is delighted with this possibility and after weighing the pros and cons, decides to give it a try.

Very grateful, the baron had been very generous, giving him a small fortune.

So Percival became a traveler of the seas, with short intervals on land.

On his floating dwellings and amidst the waves of the generous, deep sea that offers him work and food, he continues to face constant challenges, whether from heavy storms or from the mishaps that are part of his new life.

– "How many unknown lives will exist in the depths of these waters?" – He wonders, as he watches the marine movements, the constant rocking of the boats, the birds flying in search of food, the dolphins and whales surfacing and diving, intelligent and beautiful.

He is grateful for the circumstances and live his life with honesty, joy and good disposition, together with his colleagues.

Sometimes you feel homesick...

– "Everyone feels it, when they are far away, but it is not always possible to be with friends..." – he finally concludes.

The roar of the rough waters lulls him and sends his thoughts to the beautiful women he meets in every port. When will you really connect with the one who will steal your heart once and for all? I can't even imagine.

For now everything is going very well...

✳ ✳ ✳

And the beautiful and flourishing Florence, impoverished of human values, by good men who flee to survive or who are pushed aside, remains hostage to backward systems that compromise its legitimate progress.

How many perished and how many continue to perish, persecuted and martyred, but courageous, in the name of Truth?

Divine forerunners of the marvelous Renaissance which is already taking place, gradually, in spite of all the cowards and weaklings!

What is of the Law shall be fulfilled, above anyone's will.

You, Aristophanes, like so many others, are only a stone in the path of good and legitimate progress, which sooner or later will be set aside.

One day, all modified from the core, we will understand each other and together we will walk the same paths!

Finally, the misfortunes that led Wladimir and his son Norbert to leave Florence in no way sacrificed those who, willingly or unwillingly, were involved in the serious events.

Norbert and Brunilda's love problems, which seemed unresolved and without a future, were resolved in an unforeseen, unexpected and providential manner.

Thank heaven, the course of everything preserved the lives of Wladimir Vladosk and Norbert; just as it had happened on that day of sad memory, when they faced terrible challenges, under the cruelty of Diogenes and his men.

– Ah, if only the human creature had faith the size of a mustard seed! –

30.– STRANGE DIALOGUE

Isolde still does not know if she should go to the store, when the day of the meeting arrives... She does not ask advice from Forbes or Prudence. Both would refuse this, besides warning her about Theobald.

She will have to decide for herself and bear the consequences.

– "What should I do, enter into the danger that Theobald represents or run away from him? Embark on a risky journey or turn my back on this love? What will I do with this heart that gives me the inconceivable certainty that without him I will never be happy? I need the presence of this man and his love, even if I do not ignore the risks to which I will be exposed.

At times like this, I miss the good sense and friendship of the kind man. He would know how to guide me... However, today I must fend for myself.

Yet I feel like a bird that has ceased to fight and is inexorably being dragged into the snake's throat."

Forbes arrives happily and tells her that her bath is ready.

– Thank you... – she replies, without much enthusiasm.

– My child, what is wrong? Are you feeling any physical discomfort?

– Do not worry. I am fine.

– Then get ready for our tour! I will go with you! I have become accustomed to guiding you through city life!

Silently, Isolde leaves and in a few minutes returns with admirable elegance.

They leave the house and after a while they arrive at the store.

As they approach the "meeting point", Isolde shudders when she sees Theobald looking restlessly around.

Her heart races and she realizes the power this man represents in her life. Impossible to deny it. She would be very disappointed if he were not waiting for her.

With a broad smile, he approaches with a rose in his hand which he offers her, bowing in front of her nobly:

– Glad to see you, my beauty! – As he speaks, he gently takes her hand to kiss it, looking into her eyes to assess the effect of his gallantry.

Isolde shudders at the sound of his voice and the powerful effect of his gaze.

Very intrigued, Forbes asks her:

– Who is this boy, dear, do you know him?

– Yes, Forbes! It is Count Theobald of Vila D'Oro!

Forbes heard it, understood it and did not like it.

As for Theobald, he smiled very pleased, because Isolde pronounced his name.

Feigning indifference, Isolde thanked him for the rose and went to the store.

Once there, distracted, she cannot concentrate her thoughts on anything, for she feels his constant gaze.

She digs into the goods, analyzes this and that, completely disinterested.

Forbes leans closer and whispers:

– What is the matter, my daughter, do you want to go back?

– No, Forbes, do not worry so much, I am fine!

Forbes doubts what she says, but he cannot and should not contradict her. Isolde is adult and responsible.

Isolde continues her incomprehensible search for something that, if it exists, is not there. The truth is that she only wants to gain time while she decides what to do.

Theobald, while giving her space to move, gravitates around her in brazen suspense.

She feels the need to flee, but his presence is a great challenge, because it feels good and annoys her at the same time.

Finally, she chooses some accessories, just to justify her presence there.

She passes the packages to Forbes and tries to leave when Theobald approaches with determination:

– Please, precious, we need to talk, I still don't know who you are or where you live...!

– Why and what for? – She asks him.

Gallant and full of kindness, he replies, modulating his voice with seductive accents. That's what he is used to. He is aware of his fascination:

– Don't you think it is only fair that a man wants to know about the person he is interested in? Since that day, when we met by chance, I have been trying hard to find you all over Florence! If necessary, I would move heaven and earth looking for you!

She stops, looks at him, takes a deep breath and declares:

– My name is Isolde, as I told you, and I live with my grandfather, Count Fernando of Alencar Nogueira!

Theobald rejoices, it cannot get any better than that! He knows the family, the address and the financial power they represent.

Seeing his satisfied smile, she asks curiously:

– Do you know my grandfather?

– Well, dear, who does not know Count Fernando of Alencar Nogueira?

The statement had a mixture of proud satisfaction and mockery.

– This confirms my first impression. We are on the same social level! – He exclaims resoundingly.

– What if we were not?

– Well, well! You belong to the finest flower of Florentine society!

– Could you explain yourself better?

– I am talking about social status!

– Is this very important?

– I would say, to be more precise, that it is indispensable!

– So, if I am not mistaken, social level determines everything?

– Yes! That is how we are and that's how we live! Fortunately, your life also follows the same parameters!

Isolde smiles, sarcastic and amused, while looking at Forbes who, in turn, smiles a little more than her.

– "If he only knew who he is talking to...!" – Forbes thinks, unable to stop laughing. Then she walks away from them so as not to shock the count any further.

– Did I make a joke by chance? – he asks, annoyed.

– No sir, it is just that we remembered something very funny, forgive us!

– I will forgive you if you explain to me what makes you treat a servant so intimately!

– The fact that she is so much more to me! Why? Don't you have any friends?

– I do, and many! Yet of my level! – he says with great pride, as he fixes his pupils, in reproach, on Forbes.

Isolde's heart resents, and her reason screams in her ears:

– "Stay away while there is still time!"

But who said the heart always listens to reason?

She takes a breath and says to him:

– Do you divide the world into two parts, the upper for the nobility and the lower for the riffraff? – She accentuates the last word, as she looks at him defiantly.

– Well, well, it has been like that since the beginning of time! And it will always be like this! Everyone in their place! That way, everything will work out just fine!

– For whom?

– For us, of course! Those who support and lead this world with strength and intelligence!

– Ah...! I see... – she says, before asking him, very curious:

– Tell me, please, when you first saw me, what did you think?

Pleased with the direction of the conversation, he replies, giving an affectionate accent to his voice:

– And how could I think when my heart seized me dazzled by your beauty and fascination?

– Yet how could you define me in terms of your social division?

As Forbes laughs uncontrollably, Isolde keeps a quiet, wary look on her face.

Making a great effort not to burst out laughing, Forbes vibrates with the courage with which Isolde conducts the dialogue.

Theobald immediately notices the intelligent and challenging comments of his interlocutor, but wants to take advantage of the opportunity.

Isolde, looking at him, insists:

– So, what do you say?

– What more could I say to you that I have not already said? Is it possible that a star shining in the sky can disguise its luminous power? Your noble origin and your place in the heavens of the mighty are evident in this beautiful and flourishing city!

In the face of such arrogance and idiocy, prejudice and blatant ambition, Isolde concludes:

– "If you only knew, "illustrious" Count Theobald, with whom you were talking that day! Well, well, what fun it would be to show him my mansion, my wealth and my coats of arms! But who knows, someday I will have this pleasure! Life is full of surprises!"

Forbes approaches again and concludes regretfully:

– "Your heart struggles between reason and emotion... Poor sweetheart... Only God can help you..."

But Panderva continues to challenge him:

– My dear sir, if I were someone with nothing who lives on the streets, how would you behave with me?

Surprised and not understanding her, Theobald replies:

– But fortunately, you are not! Given your heraldry. Why this strange question and such absurd assumptions?

– Just to evaluate the ambition, pride and arrogance of our society...

He feels he is at a dead end. He does not understand anything.

– Are you mute, dear Count?

– And how not to be? How can such a beautiful, refined and rich girl have such strange philosophies? I confess that I don't understand your intention!

– Well, don't you go to meetings where such topics are so common? Don't you like riddles?

– It does not seem to me to be the case! The beautiful lady only challenges me, certainly to amuse herself! However, I would like you to be more explicit in what you want.

Theobald, despite his interest, sounds a bit bitter.

– Me? Nothing! The one who seems to want something is you! After all, what do you expect from me?

– To know you better and be part of your life!

– Going fast, huh? – she asks.

– Not so fast! Do not forget how long I have been looking for your beautiful and kind person! From the first moment I saw you, I was very interested and decided to conquer you!

– Ah...! You "decided" to conquer me...! You talk about conquests and I would like to know more about you!

– Oh my god! I just met an intelligent and defiant woman! I thought the fairer sex only understood about hats and vanity! – he says while he approaches her.

Silently, subtly she walks away as she analyzes her intellectual and spiritual deficiency. She deplores him from the depths of her soul. Time passed and he learned nothing... No, she is not interested.

It would be like taking refuge in a dark and dangerous cave, full of reptiles and dirt... Remember your dear friend, kind, and understand his scruples about this man.

She makes a decision and declares emphatically:

– Dear Count Theobald, please know that I am absolutely not interested in you! Have a good day!

In shock, he listened, but did not understand.

He tries to argue, but Isolde hurriedly pulls Forbes and goes to the carriage waiting for them nearby.

Theobald, open mouthed, freezes. He is aware that she is all he wants for his life.

He did not understand the challenges, and even less the outbursts. As she gets into the vehicle without looking back, he decides that he will pursue her tenaciously. Nothing will stop him, not even death...! He is still unaware of the resources he has to always get what he wants!

Thus, without knowing, Isolde increased in the heart of that stubborn man the decision to have her for himself.

Forbes asks her no questions. She follows her silently and leaves her immersed in her thoughts...

– "There they are: the Panderva of before and today, merged into one and much more experienced. Only she alone will be able to decide her own life...

However, I fear two factors interfere with this: the ruthless obstinacy of Theobald and the impudent fascination he exerts over her" – Forbes concludes, very worried.

Once home, Isolde struggles between the certainty that she got rid of someone who would probably bring her torment and the almost uncontrollable urge to go back, consenting to take back what was lost in space and time.

Upset and at the same time relieved to have done what she did, she emerges into her conflicts that only she can understand and resolve...

How many times had she felt this way? It is hard to know for sure. Since she looked around her, uncertainty, fear and pain were part of her little life. Minerva intensified her suffering.

She had been exploited and was often unsure of what she was doing and what she was supposed to do as she acted under orders and beatings.

– "Where will this woman be?!" – She wonders.

She is afraid to see her again. Minerva has the strange power to weaken her. When she sees her, she shudders and panics, although at another time and in other circumstances...

Deplorable conditioning...!

– She does not know that Minerva has already entered the spirit world and has probably already come face to face with her guilty conscience –.

– "One day I will be free of you, Minerva, forever...!" – She thinks, while another thought makes a counterpoint: if they still don't understand each other, they will have to meet again, many times. She knows, even if she wants to forget, that, if Minerva hurt her so much, and with such fury, she probably had strong ties with her. What gives her this certainty? She does not know. These are truths that are felt in her soul.

Thinking of Theobald, he reflects again:

– "If I know who he is and what he will do, what am I to do, if this love has never left me, in spite of everything?"

Prudence comes and finds her sitting in the garden meditating. With an open book in her hands and a distant gaze...

– Daughter, what's wrong with you? You came back so sad! In fact, you came back so upset! Can you tell me what happened? Can we talk?

Sighing, she disagrees:

– No, I am sorry!

– Based on my experience and remembering your mother's reactions, I can appreciate that your heart is confused!

– Yes, you are right... And, by the way, Prudence, I am very curious to know about my father. Who is he? You, my mother's maid and confidant, you must have known him!

Prudence shudders.

– So, Prudence, are you going to tell me?

– Nothing, daughter! Your mother made me swear never to tell anyone! After all, he was an unknown and irresponsible "illustrious"! Just as many others do, who disappeared without a trace!

Prudence kisses her and walks away, putting an end to the conversation. Isolde walks through the alleys of the garden, breathing the balsamic air of the plants and flowers, thinking, thinking...

Her little dog follows her, prancing.

31.– USELESS SEARCH

Under the impact of the disappearance of Norbert, Brunilda, Lucy, the coachman Percival, Wladimir Vladosk and more recently Lucy's parents: Baron Harald and his wife Bertha, curiosity increases, as well as the most diverse assumptions, which in turn led to talk about other missing persons. Although these are not well known to most, they are obviously part of the statistics of the "mysteriously missing" of Florence.

Some, aware of the political and social reality, as well as the suffocating religious reality, undeniably suspect that they are trapped in some dungeon or have already been killed.

As for Brunilda's disappearance, her maid, not discreet at all, suggested the possibility that the young woman might have a boyfriend. This was enough for more speculation, as the baron's daughter was already officially engaged to a friend of her father. The rumors spread not only to the different departments of Florence, but also to neighboring towns.

After all, the protagonists are too important to go unnoticed.

Those who admired and cared for Wladimir and Norbert sincerely regretted the absence of two such competent and helpful professionals, who bravely faced difficulties for the sake of truth.

Those who benefited from the goodness and kindness of Wladimir and Norbert, when they defended them in a legal matter and won with commitment, respect and kindness, now know that they are at the mercy of fate.

From a distance, Wladimir and Norbert, aware of this harsh reality and consequence, put everything in God's hand, who will open the way for them, even if they have to go through countless setbacks, due to the tyranny of the regime, the lack of education, proper instruction and guidance that almost always explain the misery that prevails among the less favored.

They trust because they know that the world belongs to the children of God and wherever they are, they will always receive his mercy.

Aristophanes daily records completely unequal information about the "fugitives," as he calls Wladimir's family.

Angry, he is sure that his archenemies, in addition to stealing his chance for revenge – for what, Aristophanes...? –, took with them his "pot of gold." No doubt Brunilda is with them.

He took some unfair measures – he himself admits it – with regard to his enemies who remained in Florence to challenge his authority. as a cruel criminal, he had no difficulty in punishing them ruthlessly.

Without problems of conscience, Aristophanes does his part and after each victory over the enemies of his holy Mother Church and the State, at the same time, he celebrates himself and earns more credits and praise, striving more and more to satisfy the majority and preserve the power he holds.

Proud to occupy a position of such relevance and brilliance! He would never know how to live any other way. He needs to renew more and more of the praises he receives, in addition, of course, to the actual payment to which he is "justified."

At that point, he analyzes the latest events:

"Just after the uproar caused by Don Anastacio and just when I resume my usual activities, I am surprised by these abominable mishaps! However, may all those who think of escaping wait for me! I will find them, sooner or later, wherever they are, because this world has become too small for all of us!"

He madly intensifies the search, not only in Florence, but in more distant places.

However, exhausted and maddened by hatred, he sees the days and months pass by, monotonously, without a single clue.

Possession, roars:

– It seems as if the earth swallowed them up!

Clenching his eyes that glow with hatred, he concludes accurately:

– Something tells me that beauty made of gold is with that cheerful, arrogant lawyer! Besides running away, they took away my greatest dream to be happy and increase my power! May my imprecations and curses reach them wherever they are, as I predict the bliss of having them in my hands, faster than they imagine!

Raising his voice and with his clenched fist, he announces:

– We will still face off, "defenders of the law"! – He spits aside, extremely displeased –. And when that happens, you will ask the devil to take you away to escape my madness!

He smiles sadly, strokes his neatly groomed beard and whispers:

– As for that gorgeous blonde beauty, you wasted no time! You proud, ungrateful woman! You deliberately rejected me! The girl knows how to play her cards...!

Smiling grimly, he adds, looking dreamy and greedy:

– I appreciate audacity in such a woman! I want this Germanic goddess for myself! She will brighten and color my weary, sad life, and my tormented mind will rest with your worries, while you sweeten my heart!

Sarcastic, he whispers:

– If I have a heart...!

Then he exclaims:

– I will search for her tirelessly, and even if she is in hell, I will bring her out of there! And woe to those who cross my path... The devil himself will not dare to intervene!

He had long ago noticed, extremely displeased, the glances exchanged between Brunilda and Norbert.

Neither, however, suspected his observation. Continuing his revolt, he concludes:

– You rascals...! You wasted no time...!

Ruminating his hatred, Aristophanes intensifies the spontaneous aversion he feels for the two.

Ever since he saw Wladimir and Norbert for the first time, he hated them instantly. He has regretted countless times having rescued them from Diogenes.

"Today they would no longer exist...! What a great fortune for my soul! Ah, if only I could go back in time! Norbert would not have become that abominable lawyer who torments us as much as his father, who himself would have long since returned to dust! But when I saw my opponent there, lying on the sidewalk, my hatred for him was greater and more urgent! I clumsily lost the wonderful opportunity to get them out of my way once and for all...! If that had happened, I would possibly already be married to the beautiful Brunilda!

They may have a promised future to cling to but they cannot even imagine what awaits them further down the road... Nobody stands in my way...

Anyway, it is too late now and I need to find them!"

32.– THE REINITIATION

In the distance, Wladimir and Norbert engage in an affectionate dialogue:

– Son, when I received the supposed missive from Ivo of Santorini, I immediately understood that you were telling me where you were and giving me news. Can you imagine how much I suffered, son, ignoring your whereabouts and suspecting in terror that something bad might have happened to you?

– Yes, I also suffered a lot. This urgent circumstance led me to flee without plans and without destination to save our lives and free Brunilda from a disastrous marriage, arbitrarily decided by her father, the baron.

– On leaving Florence, Norbert, I confess to you that I deeply regretted leaving that city so promising and so dear to my heart.

– I understand, my father, and I fully harmonize with your feelings.

However, raising his head, Wladimir concluded very emotionally:

– Anyway, here we are, together and united, for a new stage of life, which will undoubtedly be similar to the one we just left, since we are the same wherever we go!

Hugging him, Norbert declares:

– This is my father! Philosopher, metaphysician, doctor of law and humanist! How much I admire you! Poor humanity, subjected to so many rotten and rusty powers that impose themselves, taking lives and paralyzing progress, maintaining their anachronistic and cruel institutions! Good examples and ethical education will be the philosopher's stone of all times and of all alchemy! Only then will we have the hope of a grandiose and ever higher future!

– Well, well, the son who calls me a philosopher, besides being a philosopher, exhibits an admirable power to educate! Why don't you dedicate yourself to this task? While we take care of the new life, exercising the trade that has always characterized our family, we need the other functions, according to our real academic background.

Very excited, Norbert comments:

– Once again, my father reads in my soul like an open book! In this respect, I have already taken some steps. I will be a professor of legal justice. I am just waiting for confirmation from the institutions to which I applied.

– I congratulate you! You too in everything you do direct your moral and intellectual activities for good and truth.

– I learned this from the cradle! I always had great examples!

They both smile and embrace as they enter the house.

From the radiant country that is Italy, Wladimir departed for the cradle of culture, the luminous Greece, where he was reunited with his son and Brunilda, on the island of Santorini, where his deceased friend Ivo used to live. Without delay, they made other trips, in order to put a reasonable distance between them and their persecutors.

The persecution is carried out, not only by the powerful tentacles of the Holy Office, but also by two fierce and very interested enemies: Baron Odorico Von Braun, who will never resign himself to having lost his daughter at the hands of his enemies, and the obsessive and enigmatic Aristophanes.

Renouncing old appearances and elegant Florentine fashion, Wladimir, Norbert and Brunilda are practically unrecognizable. Wherever they arrive, the undeniable body of knowledge and competence opens every door for them.

In a new reality of life and far from "their place", Wladimir makes a comment:

– Unintentionally, I resumed the itinerant life of my gypsy ancestors!

– Are you a descendant of gypsies? – asks Brunilda.

– Yes, daughter, and with great honor! We come from the ancient and mysterious Romania. Other more distant relatives were from Bulgaria and others from Prussia. I think I inherited from this past an easier understanding of other cultures and a different *modus vivendi*.

– The life of the gypsies fascinates me! – She declares excitedly.

– Many of us must have gone through these cultural experiences. I admire their gifts for music, dance and divination. I, however, prefer what is more permanent! I live better with the certainty of the present and the planned future, which does not mean that I have not done well in this way of life! After all, we are made of the same clay, malleable and subjected to numerous adaptations. – Norbert declares.

– In this way of life, I wonder how much learning and how much beauty there is to enjoy, not to mention the mishaps of every existence and the clashes of passions, so common in these peoples!

They have to face literally and almost always great storms: from the weather or from their own organizations! – Brunilda reflects.

– In the face of life's storms, we become strong! – Wladimir says.

– Yes! Over the millennia, man has learned to defend himself and to work, step by step, for his survival and well-being! – Brunilda adds.

– From the beginning of our existence, which is lost in the memory of time, man has faced his tragedy and his glory in order to survive, acting almost always in defense of what he thinks he has, although he has to leave it on countless occasions to others who, momentarily, are the "winners." So, he learned to defend and hunt, to feed and protect himself from threats. We know this story well, but we rarely think about it, as if we had already encountered everything that exists on the planet and the advances that intelligences have invented.

Passions, in turn, have been transformed over time, but they still dominate us and, according to different levels of understanding, they subdue us or serve as a lever for intellectual and moral growth.

Gypsies and other peoples, even remnants, almost pure, in different tribes, strong and determined, in their actions and will, are still bathed in dramatic and imposing actions. We know stories of love, hate, revenge and death, in the face of rivalries and hierarchies, gypsy or tribal, almost always uncontrollable.

Norbert pauses and concludes:

– Anyway, taking away the excesses of all cultures, including our own, how much beauty this world holds! We, aestheticians by choice, feel in the depths of our souls a unique admiration for all forms of beauty and harmony.

– I appreciate the gypsies' clothes, their ornaments, the strength and passionate vibe they exert in everything they do, the joy of their camps, their vibrant music, their fascinating dances and their musical instruments. Anyway, the reality of these people fascinates me and makes me dream with eyes open! – Brunilda bursts into a frenzy.

Delighted, Norbert smiles:

– Well, well, father! This Germanic goddess is challenging me! How to compete with such cultural richness and charm? The gypsies have found in you an advocate and an ally, my dear!

Bewildered, she almost apologizes:

– Do not be impressed, Norbert, I am like that! Extreme in my feelings and reverent to human reality, at its best! Everything that represents strength and greatness attracts and fascinates me! I do not appreciate colorless feelings! We are this or that, we want it or not, we like it or not! Certainly, a great vigilance not to exceed ourselves and to know where the healthy limits are is just and necessary, after all, we are rational and increasingly capable beings; which indicates that the responsibility for everything we do is to the extent of the knowledge of the facts. I firmly believe that few in this world who have already made any progress can honestly say that they "did not know" when they did wrong...

Saddened, Brunilda remembers her father's tragic and unforgivable way of living...

Norbert noticing this, embraced her solicitously. He is dazzled by the beautiful colors that reach this woman, as she makes her patent defenses:

– I know, my dear, the strength you carry in your veins and the power of exaltation and impetuosity of your race, which brings in itself many virtues, but also its idiosyncrasies that are ostensibly reflected in these or those characters, according to the levels of consciousness already reached.

Wherever we go, whatever our origins and ancestors, we will always be the only ones responsible for ourselves and our actions, before God, the world and our neighbor. In short, nothing and no one will serve us as a defense resource or as an excuse for mistakes, whatever they may be!

Knowing that you know this, I understand that you fear for the consequences that will henceforth come to your father as an effect of his actions! Rest your little heart, giving it to heaven!

– "I already do that, Norbert...". My father's temperament reveals a force as destructive, as intemperate as uncontrollable. He himself resembles the terrible earth storm...!

– Do not be like that, Brunilda, one day your father will learn, even if it is through suffering!

– He and all those who act in the same way! – She confirms.

Addressing his father who listens attentively, Norbert clarifies:

– Despite leaving everything behind, which will never be easy for anyone, Brunilda got rid of the prison and the torments inflicted on her by her father. That man beat her cruelly, even wounding her many times. From those occasions she has some scars.

– We know these cases very well. In the Forum, how many times we come across facts like these! It is unfortunate to see that the law approves and strengthens this behavior, which makes it difficult to defend these unhappy children – Wladimir confirms.

Brunilda raises her head and confesses:

– In fact, I regret my father's way of being, despite my best efforts, he gradually became one less reason to exist. Motherless from an early age, I still remember missing her sweet presence in my life!

But, in spite of everything I have lived through, especially after her, how can I deny that my life did have its charms? In all phases I was as happy as I could be.

I always get the best out of everything! Resources have always allowed me to travel a lot, to meet other countries and other people. Art and culture have always been within my reach. Thus, I became enlightened as much as I wanted. My father, proud of his daughter, encouraged me and rewarded me with the most extraordinary opportunities... He takes that credit.

Wladimir concludes:

– Above all differences, we are all similar creatures with the same destiny on the face of this tiny planet. On this evolutionary path, we are on our way to the desired perfection. Different levels of learning are formed here and there. Struggling learners reach happiness sooner, while others trudge along, unprotected, angry and lazy. However, the Creator forgets no one and all will arrive, sooner or later, because this journey has no end. It is our human condition to be perfect one day. That is what we are here for and we are on a pilgrimage through this tiny world that is part of a complex of bigger and better ones, under the fulfillment of natural laws.

Brunilda thinks of their enemies who never get tired of looking for them.

Wladimir noticed that she was pensive:

– Are you sad, daughter?

– Yes, I am sorry! I cannot forget that we have fierce pursuers on our way! If they find us, this joy could end overnight! I am neither ungrateful nor insensitive; I know that the heavens abandon no one, especially those who follow their laws, but I am too human and imperfect to ignore the evil that surrounds us and that sooner than we can suppose may cause us disastrous consequences that will endanger our health and happiness! I fear, above all, that life will separate us, Norbert! If that happens, I swear, I will not be able to bear it!

With each new word or expression, Brunilda is saddened by the thought that she might again be a prisoner of her father's cruelty and that Norbert and his noble father might be accused of something that the chief persecutors know very well how to engender.

Gradually she begins to cry, snuggling close to Norbert. He holds her close to his heart, and even though he knows that what fills her thoughts with uncertainty may happen at any moment, he lovingly and confidently suggests to her:

– Do not suffer beforehand! Let us live well in this new time that blesses us with so many joys and good promises, my dear! When the future comes with its natural impositions, we will adapt ourselves to it, counting, above all, on the mercy of God, who knows all and gives all! Remember the success of our unexpected escape and how our lives were successfully resolved through it! Take it easy and enjoy the happiness of being together!

Even weeping, she listens to his wise and providential words, nodding affirmatively with her beautiful golden head.

Father and son wait for her to calm down while reflecting equally on their own lives.

How to ignore the brutal reality of the world and the vigilance and cruelty of men? They would be ostriches hiding their heads in the sand, hoping that their pursuers would not see them.

However, they are not fools and making good use of reason they know what to expect, even if they apparently do not deserve it. Merits and demerits are known only to God, who through his laws allows each one to return the blessings for the good and love experienced, or the struggle for the necessary learning, lessons to which each one is entitled, along the multiple evolutionary paths.

– Whatever happens, Brunilda, we will stay together, because our souls are inseparable! In any case, we will continue to love each other, even if we are not together! – Norbert concludes.

Straightening up, Brunilda leaves her husband's arms, stands proudly in front of them and with a strong and melodious voice exclaims:

– Peace be with us! Keep calm and heed the truth because wavering faith is like lack of faith! May we be worthy of all that we receive from God's bountiful hands! Know, for the repose of your hearts, that "what is done is done," and that divine providence will not only keep you from previous dangers, but, covering you with powerful and invisible veils, will maintain your freedom. Continue steadfastly in the good intentions you always have, wherever you are, and may you never lose the faith or the joy that must always bathe the heart of the Christian!

Go forward and never return to the old nest!

Life expects much from one and all, for "much will be asked of the one who gave much!"

Peace to your hearts, now and forever!

Brunilda is silent, shudders, sways on her feet, and supported by her husband, sits on a chair.

Norbert awaits her recovery and Wladimir, weeps submissively and thanks from the depths of his soul the heavenly powers that are always ready to help God's children, in the most unpredictable ways.

He sits down and wipes his tears as he recovers from the great emotion that overcomes him.

When Brunilda is better, Norbert approaches his father and hugs him without being able to say anything. The emotion that invades him is no less...

Brunilda admires them and is equally moved, because although she does not remember the words she said, she knows that once again the heavenly forces have used her gifts for good.

Norbert declares:

– I forgot to tell you, father, that our dear Brunilda has the same "weirdness" as Panderva, our oracle!

Smiling, satisfied and moved, Wladimir exclaims:

– Praise God! One day, these gifts will not only be investigated and respected, but also very well directed. Oh, men, when will you learn to choose only the good, in any place and in any man?

Then he says to them with affection:

– I invite you to go to our domestic prayer room and give thanks for the incomparable graces we have received today through God's mercy!

Joyful and holding each other, the three of them go to the oratory, and as they walk, intrigued and somewhat annoyed, Brunilda discreetly addresses her husband:

– I want to know who Panderva is! An old love, Norbert? – Jealous and with a penetrating gaze, she studies her husband's expressions.

Norbert bursts into laughter that disconcerts her:

– Yes!

Brunilda's eyes flash.

He is amused by this, as he declares:

– A brotherly love, my dear! Panderva was my father's protégée! Today she is with her family! We will tell you about it later, I promise!

Laughing in embarrassment, she says affectionately and already regretting her own outbursts:

– Excuse me, but emotions take over me and sometimes they take precedence over reason! Especially when it is about you...

They both smile and go to pray gratefully...

※ ※ ※

Souls like these, who have already understood the truth and follow it, make a difference in this clash of forces that worlds like ours are facing.

Walkers of the shining stars, at different levels of evolution, we seek, each in our own way, and according to our angle of vision, to carry the kingdom of heaven within us, in the highest aspiration of our souls, who, despite stepping on material ground, dream of ethereal spaces where divine greatness lives!

Sacred and human dichotomy: the heavens are outside and inside us!

※ ※ ※

After the emotions and prayers, Wladimir went to his room, while Norbert lovingly took Brunilda with him.

– Your father is a wonderful person, my love! And so wise! – She exclaims reverently.

– Yes! I am proud of it!

– You two are so alike...!

– Thank you for the compliment! My father has been my great example in life! At birth, the good fairy gave me divine gifts:

two great and loving spirits who were my parents, and then, the woman of my life, whom I found not by chance and who was born for me, living somewhere else, waiting to make me happy!

Laughing, Brunilda is amused:

– Don't forget that, at the present moment, evil geniuses also assisted intruders in your group, and you introduced fierce enemies to her!

Laughing likewise, he concludes:

– Before the philosophy of life that I have received from the cradle, these are our best teachers! With them we learn in any way and at any time! They are a fatality in this world, after all, they almost always represent our past debts!

– Wise as your father! I hope that our children will inherit this intelligence and elevation of thoughts!

– Which also characterize their future mother, plus an incomparable beauty that also has its value, especially on Earth!

In love, they kiss and exchange caresses, enraptured.

In his office, Wladimir gives free rein to his inspirations and writes, uninterruptedly, extracting from his own essence the glittering gems of wisdom that he transmits to paper, oblivious to the reality around him.

Humble by nature, he considers these notes to be exercises in metaphysical learning.

Moments ago, his beloved daughter-in-law, who enriched his life so much more and brought longed-for happiness to his son, had been a loving messenger of comforting premonitions.

They will continue with their life as they wish, always adapting themselves to divine providence, which will wisely grant them all that they need and not only what they long for.

Accustomed always to fulfill his obligations, while living and exercising his life in the best way, he will continue to do so, as long as God permits him.

When he leaves the world, he hopes to say goodbye peacefully and momentarily to his son and his family, in the certainty of new encounters to resume the love that characterizes and strengthens them in their different journeys, wherever they are. Their moral and affective achievements will always be kept and preserved as identifying jewels, to be recognized in any part of the Universe, amalgamating and at the same time liberating their happy and fraternal souls.

This is how the children of God, the Creator, must live in this immeasurable Universe!

33.– THE GREAT REVOLT OF THEOBALD

In Florence, our ex-queen, involved in Theobald's love – Genebaldo in the past –, decides not to resist any more and to try again.

This man, intelligent and experienced, did everything to get closer to her and ended up winning her heart.

Thinking of the inexorability of time and the longing for life, in what she considers sacred; that is, to form a family and try to be happy, she accepted his marriage proposal, without deceiving herself; however, as to the character of the one who, in spite of everything, remains her great love.

Her soul, which has suffered from an early age facing the great challenges of life, concludes that she must fight for a new experience, giving herself the opportunity to readapt.

Then, between ups and downs, doubts and hopes, Isolde accepts and assumes the engagement.

With much effort she obtained her grandfather's approval, as he had already had several altercations with Genebaldo.

Fernando, despite his apparent consent, is determined to eliminate once and for all Isolde's suitor, whom he labels "dishonorable", as much as the one who made his beloved Carlota unhappy. Thus, he plunges into schisms and conflicts, becoming distant and silent.

Seeing him restless in the halls, during the hours that should be dedicated to physical and mental rest, in mysterious soliloquies, has become very common.

He has already warned his beloved granddaughter on countless occasions, but she, independent by nature, ignores his warnings because she is completely caught in the boy's fascination.

Without reacting against her grandfather, Isolde maintains her plans to marry her fiancé. She is not unaware of the abyss she is heading for.

Deep down, physically and spiritually, Fernando is in a very worrying state.

Finding him pacing restlessly in the garden, Isolde decides to speak to him once more:

– My dear grandfather, sit here with me on this bench! Why do you torment yourself so much?

She sits down, breathes noisily and says:

– Why do you ask me what you already know?

– I was hoping you would calm down in time!

– Calm down? You do not know what you are asking me! How can I watch you walk to perdition and do nothing?

– Does not the fact that you know I love Theobald tell you anything?

– It certainly does! And that is what torments me the most! How could anyone be happy with a man like him?!

– If I did not think I could be happy with him, I would have not accepted I his request for marriage!

– Poor daughter... You are blind...! – He stammers, making her granddaughter sad.

Fernando gets up agitated and answers:

– You will never be happy with Theobald!

– What makes you so sure?

– Knowing how he is and how he acts! Around you he plays the role of a good boy, deceiving you!

– Grandfather, don't you think I can change him?

Almost in despair, Fernando takes her hands, looks deeply into her eyes and laments:

– Poor darling... How naive! Who told you I would allow it? With him, your life will be hell!

Isolde feeling hurt asks him:

– Do not say that, I beg you! Do not increase my torments any more...!

"She also imagines what she will face... Then why...?" – He thinks, while his granddaughter is already on the verge of tears.

Already regretting having said too much, he embraces her and pleads:

– Forgive me! Forget everything I told you! Don't take me seriously, I beg you!

He kisses her and leaves quickly.

Intimately, he has already made up his mind. He will face heaven and earth, but Isolde will not marry Theobald.

The amorous sufferings of his daughter were enough for him and his beloved granddaughter has already suffered too much during a single life.

Prudence approaches and consoles Isolde, while warning:

– Daughter, your grandfather is a very mysterious person and will do whatever he wants, regardless of any other wishes!

– Why are you telling me this, Prudence?

– I cannot explain it to you, forgive me! – Saying this, she walks away.

In silence, Isolde confirms, once again, that this family is very mysterious and must hide many secrets... She is afraid for her grandfather and for Theobald... What will come...?!

The next day, Fernando urgently calls the boy to talk to him alone.

Deeply annoyed, he accepts the invitation but arrives with a frown on his face:

– What do you want from me, Count?

– We both know what I want! Do not make a fool of yourself! We know each other too well for that! Leave my granddaughter in peace!

Bold and mocking, Theobald confronts him:

– Well, well, I am good as a party companion, but I am not good to be your relative! Is that it? Since when did you become a moralistic mocker?

Fernando turns red, such is his anger. Silently, he continues to stare at him, waiting for an answer.

– No, I will never stay away from her! Believe me if you want, but I love your granddaughter!

– And since when did you learn to love? Your path is made of irresponsibility and unlove! Understand that I will never allow you to make my granddaughter unhappy!

– I promise to make her happy!

With a strange laugh, Fernando responds ironically:

– And what else do you promise? To be a good, respectful and loving companion?! Do not make me laugh!

– I promise you anything you want, as long as you allow our wedding! After all, Isolde and I are adults and we do not need your approval!

– What approval are you talking about? Are you forgetting that the law gives me inalienable rights over my granddaughter? It depends on my consent!

More and more annoyed, Theobald explodes:

– Don't you see that she loves me too? Why do you want to prevent us from being happy?

– Is it for this love that you get drunk day after day in the most sordid places of the city?

Caught by surprise, Theobald informs him hopefully:

– When we marry, I will leave this bohemian life, after all you know very well that every man has his most urgent needs!

Looking at him with a hatred so great that it leaves no room for doubt about what he thinks, Fernando looks at him in silence.

Theobald confronts him and asks impatiently:

– Well! What do you intend? To challenge me to a duel? It would be as much fun to knock you down without effort, as to cut a dry branch! Give up! Nothing and no one will prevent me from marrying Isolde!

Fernando then decides:

– "I will play my last card and may Isolde forgive me, since I know I should not...!"

Without taking his eyes off his opponent, he peremptorily orders:

– Sit down and make yourself comfortable!

– What for, we have said all we had to say!

– You are wrong! Listen to me and do not interrupt me! I will tell you about Panderva's life!

Mockingly, Theobald comments:

– Well, well, the lord count is getting senile! Who is Panderva and why would I be interested in her?

– I assure you that you know her well and that you will soon understand me. So, shut up and listen to me!

Fernando begins to tell him everything and especially the fact that when he met her, she was still wandering the streets, without resources. For this, she should be despised by him and by the nobility in general.

Theobald, little by little, understands and suffers an impact that is difficult to measure.

His thoughts go back to that day and he remembers that, in fact, she was standing alone!

He remembers again the day they saw each other in the tent and the first two meetings, and understands her defiant manner in talking to him, as well as her kindness and intimacy with the maid... He understood, furious, her ironic tirades and mocking laughter...

– "How much fun she must have had at my expense...! But in spite of everything, I can feel her sincere affection and interest... Her eyes do not deceive me... But, then, why didn't she tell me everything as Count Fernando is doing now? She was certainly afraid I would reject her!"

If I was not sitting down, I would have to...

The count knows him quite well and knows his unshakable pride.

He reasons and retorts quickly:

— However, my dear Count, if anyone here is worthy of a fair admonition, it is you, who was even ignorant of the existence of this granddaughter!

— What I did or do is none of your business!

— You say so while judging me in this way! This means that our little Countess Isolde has already wandered the streets of Florence and... who knows with whom, right? How dare she be part of the nobility with a past like this?!

The count clenches his fists and controls himself not to advance towards him, as it would be useless as well as dangerous. Theobald has committed several crimes and all "legal..."

He only stammers, furiously:

— My granddaughter is pure as an angel, despite all she has lived through! She learned to live and survive like no one else!

— This is what frightens me! What would she have done to survive? What is more, dear Count: is she really your granddaughter? How can you be sure? As you can see, you cannot even prove her lineage!

For all his fury, Count Fernando realizes he has hit the bull's eye. That man will never give up his pride and vanity. He counts on that.

Theobald goes from an extreme pallor to a more intense reddening. By the end of that meeting, he is anchored to the ground and cannot speak.

So angry is he that he did not even see when, smiling grimly, Isolde's grandfather walked away without looking back.

On the way, Fernando is fully aware of what he has done.

He dangerously exposed his granddaughter's life.

However, he rejoices to see Theobald perplexed, disappointed and disillusioned, pacing back and forth.

When he arrived home, he found his granddaughter.

Surprised by his nervousness, Isolde asks him:

– What happened, grandfather?

Hugging her emotionally, he replies:

– I just went for a walk to relax!

Panderva, in her heart, feels that her grandfather did much more than just go for a walk...

Walking towards the entrance of the mansion, he stops, turns to his granddaughter and declares:

– You really do not know your "fiancé"!

– Maybe I do, Grandpa...

– Impossible! If you did, you would run away from him like a contagious disease!

Deeply distressed, she concludes that her attempt to be happy is probably being aborted...

As her grandfather heads for the doorway of the house, she remains seated, not knowing what to do.

Then Forbes comes looking for her. She sits down beside her, hugs her affectionately and whispers words of affection.

The two remain in each other's arms, while Isolde weeps until she has let it all out.

A few days later, Felizardo fell ill and, despite care and treatment, ended up exhaling in his owner's arms, never taking his eyes off her, until his blurred vision revealed that he was no longer part of the world.

Isolde mourned him as she would mourn the loss of a good and dear friend. This little animal had been, for many years, her best companion, the most present, the most faithful.

✳ ✳ ✳

These little brothers of ours, who exist and contribute to the improvement of their own life, are part of the divine creation, which has an equal purpose, as to their existence in this and other worlds.

One day, they will be better understood, respected and loved, when man's reason will be enlightened to understand that everything that exists in the world is part of creation, which must and should be respected and preserved, within our possibilities, for the physical and spiritual balance of the world and the universe.

Angry! Very brave! For these beings who contribute to the progress of human beings, loving and supporting them in their different activities.

Not infrequently, in imperfect worlds like ours, the "brutal", still hostage of his own instincts, behaves better and with more nobility than certain men who, as humans, seem to have only the appearance.

God created us simple and ignorant and we have been so many times!

Everything evolves. Nothing is improvised.

Created one day to reach perfection, we walk the paths of progress and liberation.

✳ ✳ ✳

Entering the house, like a wild and uncontrollable bull, Theobald, furious at having made a mistake, does not even reflect on the feelings he has for Isolde...

Walking, restless and thirsty for revenge, he thinks, plots and refines intentions into the worst that his dark soul can engender.

Matthew had already been expelled, as had others, when they tried to serve him, as they usually do. Some were beaten and kicked without explanation.

So, Theobald spent hours pondering alone and somberly, his revolt and the decision to do something about it...

"Ah! How much you must have enjoyed yourself at my expense, perfidious woman! That is what you are! A woman with a dubious past that no man would want to espouse! Today you pose as a noblewoman, exhibit skill and finesse in society! Oh, what a mistake!

How false! If the Count had not revealed her past to me, I would fall into the trap of this shameless woman! Wait for me, you idiot! I will turn you into a rag with which I will clean my boots! I will catch you, one way or another! I will have you for myself! You will finally meet the real Count Theobald of Vila D'Oro and you will regret, each new day, having deceived me as you did. You will bitterly regret having crossed my path!"

Matthew's heart is suspended; his boss reveals a fury that promises great storms and everyone will suffer the consequences, anyway and in the worst way. Theobald spares no one and no one and passes over everything! Nothing is sacred to him!

He would like to know where his good friend Cyrene is... After his disappearance, he felt lonelier...

Time has already caught up with him, inexorably, and his strength fails him when he least expects it...

Soon he will be cast aside, when he is no longer useful, or he will be thrown into the street, without mercy... This happens every day to those who, like him, have nothing of their own, no relatives...

He spends his nights crying and lamenting his life. Meanwhile, Theobald plans a way to get Isolde in his power. He will do it in the most mysterious way possible. No one will suspect him or anyone in his service...

"I will not hire anyone... It is safer.

Fernando loves his granddaughter to veneration and will be furious if he suspects me ... "

After many sleepless nights, he decides on a risky action. "Well, it won't be the first time I dare to do these adventures, worthy of a real man! It will be great to have you at my feet, as a lover, docile and prisoner of my will! No one will suspect as I will give her "royal lodgings"! We will be a couple! Yes, we will! In my way, of course...!"

In the midst of a guffaw, he plans a venture that only he knows.

So, he dresses in black, puts on tight clothes, a hood over his head, ropes around his waist and with an iron will decides to kidnap Isolde, at night and in silence. To do this, he takes a bottle of narcotic to render her unconscious before taking her away.

At dawn, a sepulchral silence, he sneaks near the walls of the mansion and climbs the walls, stealthily.

He leaves two sentries unconscious, overcomes the first barriers and advances in the direction of his desire, orienting himself in the spaces around the rooms of Isolde and her usual companions, Forbes and Prudence.

However, he does not know that Count Fernando, knowing him well and expecting reprisals on his part, watches attentively and accompanied by his faithful servant Heraclitus, a truculent man and fond of fights.

Hiding in some bushes, Fernando watches his granddaughter's room.

Suddenly, he sees a figure he immediately recognizes and informs Heraclitus, telling him what to do.

Muy intrigado, el criado revela que reconoció a Theobald, pero Fernando le indica que debe continuar con la acción y le hace un gesto ordenándole que lo mate.

Very intrigued, the servant reveals that he recognized Theobald, but Fernando tells him that he must continue with the action and makes a gesture ordering him to kill him.

Heraclitus comes out like a silent snake, approaches Theobald without being noticed, and at a short distance, throws him a sharp dagger without even giving him time to scream.

Theobald slips, hits some walls and collapses to the ground with a thud.

Agile, like a cat, Heraclitus lifts the tall, slender body of the young man.

In a cart he takes it out of the city and, far away, disposes of the body, returning alone the next afternoon, tired and grim-faced.

On arrival, he informs his boss of what he has done and goes to his room.

Matthew, who noticed Theobald's absence, warned the family that he had been tirelessly searching for him all over Florence.

Count Theobald of Vila D'Oro became one of the missing, adding to the burden of fear and mystery... When simple people disappear, no one notices or comments, but when several prominent personalities begin to disappear without a trace, the act arouses much curiosity.

Speculation increases with each new day, and decreases when other disappearances occur. After all, everyone is minding their own business.

In Isolde's heart there is great disappointment.

Upon learning of the disappearance of her fiancé, she became suspicious of her grandfather and grew sad...

She mourned Theobald and kept him in her heart, praying for his soul, for he is probably no longer alive.

What would her friend, the good man, think if he knew what had happened? But even he will not be able to help her, distant as he is...

Fernando, realizing his granddaughter's sadness, who lonely misses her fiancé, becomes more and more depressed and that strong and willing man, who one day sought her tirelessly to comfort his beloved daughter, fades little by little.

A month later, on a cloudy and sad afternoon, Isolde buried, amidst disconsolate tears, the one who had given her a name and a real family.

After the loss of her grandfather, she fell gravely ill and hovered between life and death.

Forbes and Prudence joined forces to rescue her. Finally, after some time, Isolde overcame her physical and spiritual difficulties and survived.

She lovingly had a small statue of Felizardo made and placed in the garden, right at the entrance, amidst a beautiful clump of tiny white flowers.

When sadness overwhelms her, she sits next to "Felizardo" and remembers the past...

At this moment, Prudence and Forbes find her so far away from reality, looking at the blue sky full of very white clouds.

– Daughter! – Forbes steps forward –. What are you doing there all alone?

They both sit down, one on each side, and make it clear that they have some intention.

– Daughter, the hardest things in your life are gone, thank heaven, and you need to look at this new time! – Prudence declares, lovingly.

– We have both been talking about your life, my dear – Forbes says.

– Have you? And what have you "decided" this time, huh? – She asks playfully.

Forbes continues to expand on the ideas that, according to her, belong to both of us:

– We think of life as being made up of good days and bad days; of times of pain and times of joy. So you need to think about yourself, after so many years of struggle and hardship!

– And what do you suggest?

– Pay attention, daughter! You are beautiful as a rosebud! If it didn't work out with the one you wanted, another one can make you happy! There are good men, believe me, who have great intentions! After all, life happens and, in time, you will be older and less excited about life and the future you may have!

Laughing, Isolde wants to know:

– Which of the two has already been married and has experience in this sector?

They both look at each other and Forbes answers, stern and objective, as always:

– Isolde, it is not necessary, many times, having gone through the same experiences is enough to know the outcome, because the world is there teaching us just around the corner!

Isolde agrees:

– You are right... But those who lived or those who still live like me, know how cruel and unfair the world can be when we meet bad people...! But I recognize that I didn't learn it all by myself! My oasis, you know, I found it in the house of the dear kind man! May he be a thousand times blessed and protected wherever he goes! Him and his son Norbert!

This allusion to the two made Forbes get excited and ask:

– Where and how will they both be...! How I miss them!

– And I am sure they will miss us too!

– Yes, I am sure...

Giving them each a kiss, Isolde walks away.

A strange anxiety settles in her heart and she decides to check her "place" one more time...

He dresses simply and leaves with that intention, regretting the absence of her usual companion...

She sets off in a carriage accompanied by Forbes and Prudence. As they approach the place, she gets out, asks them to wait right there and walks away.

She goes up and down hills, enters alleys that look like a labyrinth and after a while, she finally arrives.

She walks, slowly, observing everything, and being observed.

She continues to ignore the stares, recalling several life experiences there, when he suffered the setbacks created and maintained by Minerva in her usual cruelty.

When she finally reaches her little hideout, in a natural nook and cranny somewhat disguised by old destroyed walls, she finds a newborn puppy, shivering with cold and hunger, abandoned.

Look around and see no one. You conclude, wisely, that it had been left there on purpose.

She grabs her voluminous skirt, bends down and picks up the pet. She hugs it against her chest to warm it and exclaims lovingly:

– Come with me, my little friend!

Hugging him, she leaves and heads for the carriage, when a handsome man intercepts her path, smiling, very gallantly:

– Good morning, beautiful lady! How lucky is this little doggy to be on your lap! He is very lucky!

He bows very elegantly and smiles, showing perfect teeth like picked pearls.

Hat in hand, he approaches the carriage, which she tries to board and asks her:

– Can you give me some point of reference that will allow me to see you again? I look forward to it!

Prudence smiles in anticipation of seeing her consent in the proximity of such a handsome and kind young man.

Always smiling, he adds:

– Beautiful lady, I can take care of this little animal, if necessary! I specialize in veterinary medicine!

Silent, but sympathetic to his interest, Isolde replies:

– Leave me your address and if necessary I will look for you!

He hands her a small card with legible letters, which he takes out of the pocket of his elegant coat.

Bending down as he hands it to her, she whispers:

– I have never wanted to take care of a puppy so much...!

Laughing, she asks curiously:

– So do you want this poor thing to get sick?

– Certainly not! But we know that a puppy requires special care!

– Very well, I will be looking for you soon!

Having said this, she sits down next to Forbes, who gives the boy a kind smile and tells him, without words, that he can count on her help.

He bows gratefully and walks away as the coachman starts the carriage. He stands there until it disappears around the next corner.

Dreamy, he sighs, eyes shining and says to himself:

– Where have you been all this time, I am going to win your heart, I promise! You are everything I ever wanted...!

Meanwhile, Isolde, who also liked him a lot, asks Forbes dreamy:

– Did you notice, Forbes, how he looks like Theobald?

Yes, she noticed, but she does not like the subject and answers:

– No, my dear, I do not think so! If so, I would not have liked him! – She says, observing the reactions of the girl who seems enlightened.

She has not seen such joy on her face in a long time.

"Anyway, this meeting will bring good things! And if it is up to me, this little animal will need, very soon, someone very nice and competent...!"

She smiles and leans back to enjoy the ride back.

Isolde enters the house with her treasure hidden in her chest, warming it with love.

As she walks, she concludes happily:

– Ah, the ways of life! Without knowing it, I went looking for my new Felizardo!

Forbes, who is right behind, adds:

– You went looking, my dear, not only for the puppy, but for a suitor and a good one!

– You are quick, eh, Forbes? – She asks amused. Forbes hugs Prudence and declares:

– Look, Isolde, look at both of us! What do you see?

– Well, two people I love too much!

– No, not only that, but two very lonely people who, if they had not found you, would be even lonelier! Do you want to stay like this? Do you think it is worth it, my daughter?

Holding the little animal, Isolde stops and responds:

– I know what you mean, Forbes, and I agree with you, believe me. But let us wait and see what life has to offer me!

– Be careful not to miss all your opportunities, my dear! Think of your dreams as a woman and do not want to live like us and so many others who never made their dreams of love come true! Do you doubt that we ever had them too?

– No, my dears, certainly not... I promise to think about what you say, okay?

The two embrace amusingly and celebrate Isolde's promise by rehearsing dance steps, making the girl laugh heartily.

They have long since ceased to compete for Isolde's love, as she distinguishes the two with equal attention and love. Isolde leaves and goes to meet with dignity her "new Felizardo."

34.– THE NEMESIS

The violent and ambitious Baron Odorico Von Braun, some time after the disappearance of his daughter, fell victim to a sudden illness, leaving the world and everything he loved to enter his Walhalla, without sword and without honor...

After his funeral, his future son-in-law, shamed by the society of Florence, packed his bags and returned crestfallen to his beloved Westphalia, forgetting Brunilda. The latter will never know that, for some time, in his delirium, her fiancé shared his place with another...

Mina, alone among the servants, had to put up with the relatives and heirs who seized everything that had belonged to von Braun, feeling the longing for her beloved Brunilda and Percival, whom she dreamed of with open eyes. She still sighs when she thinks of him...

Aristophanes, in turn, fought madly against all the frustrated and incomprehensible possibilities of discovering the whereabouts of Wladimir and Norbert, as well as that of the beautiful and desired Brunilda.

A few years later, his mental imbalance became patent and unbearable for those who submitted to him by hierarchy or collusion.

Interned in a hospital that belongs to his church, amidst roars and convulsive screams, bound to thick chains that hold his arms and legs, he defends himself from aggressors that only he can see.

Despised and forgotten, he suffers from hunger, thirst and all forms of need.

A few months go by, when, on a cloudy day, he wakes up without understanding anything, perplexed by his own situation, which seems like a nightmare to him, when he hears "that voice", so familiar to him, to invite him, "very kindly":

– Come, Aristophanes! The day has finally come to receive you as you deserve...! Together with us you will live everything you did to your victims! Come...!

A low moan rose in Aristophanes' throat, muffling his last unintelligible words in the grim display on his terrified face...

A nurse who faces the horrific vision, crossing herself, several times, cries out to heaven:

– Praise be to the Creator, He alone can understand and help souls like this one, dark and lost, in life or in death!

A pious priest, who is in the habit of visiting the unfortunate who end their days there, approaches and ratifies full of faith:

– Yes, daughter! Only our Lord, in his infinite mercy, can reach and understand these men who, knowing love and hatred, prefer to follow the paths of evil!

Taking the keys to the chains and locks, he himself frees Aristophanes, who in life no longer resembles a human being at all.

He makes the usual prayers and grants him the holy viaticum. Then give him to those who have the task of organizing the burial.

– Without any of the pomp to which Aristophanes was so accustomed... – The body is thrown like a bundle on a cart that is already impregnated with the smell of death, to follow the mournful path to the last resting place. The place is a little distant.

As the wheels of the vehicle squeal ominously, amid reckless curses and blasphemies from the driver, following the proper route, a series of menacing thunder and lightning begins.

In a few moments, a furious storm breaks out. Measuring the distance that still separates him from the sacred field, the driver stops, thinks and decides that he will go no further...

He throws off Aristophanes' body and pushes him disrespectfully out of the vehicle.

With a thud, the body falls to the side of the road and remains there for the vultures, who after the downpour will search for food.

When he returns to the hospital, he will say he has done his duty.

By the irony of fate, all that belonged to the brilliant and powerful Aristophanes, who had the fate of so many in his hands, and who had made them suffer and failure without any problem of conscience to enjoy all that he could profit in the world he proudly represented, is being "measured, weighed and divided" among his peers, who think they live eternally to enjoy material life without thinking of the same God they claim to represent...

EPILOGUE

Like a flowing river, life goes on, uninterrupted, here and there...

The years have turned Wladimir into a venerable old man, loved and admired by all.

Norbert, happy and fulfilled as a man and a citizen, distinguishes his existence with the best he has, together with his beloved wife and his two children, intelligent, good and worthy heirs of all the love they found when they arrived.

Brunilda, happy as a wife and devoted as a mother, became more beautiful in her maturity.

She never heard from her father again, but hopes he is in heaven. In her grateful heart she never forgot Lucy and Percival.

She hopes they are well.

Brunilda cradles in her arms a baby, who already has the great responsibility of having the same name as his great-grandfather, Wladimir, who left them a few years ago, surrounded by peace.

Norbert and Brunilda give the child to the nanny, after kissing him with much affection, and they embrace each other tightly:

– How I miss your father, my love!

– Imagine my heart, Brunilda! Live without him!

Deeply moved, Brunilda weeps and Norbert kisses her in silence. There is nothing more to say, but much to feel...

Life will go on for this one who now arrives, to complete the richness and happiness that life on Earth can bring.

And we, my dear readers, wonder rationally and lovingly:

– Is this little one arriving or returning to the arms of his loved ones?!

Chi lo sa...?

ROCHESTER

Books of Vera Kryzhanovskaia and JW Rochester

The Jew's Revenge

The Wedding Nun

The Witch's Daughter

Swamp Flower

Divine Wrath

The Legend of Montignoso Castle

The Death of the Planet

St. Bartholomew's Night

Blessed Are the Poor in Spirit

Cobra Capela

Dolores

Kingdom of the Shadows Trilogy

From Heaven to Earth

Episodes from the Life of Tiberius

Infernal Spell

Herculanum

On the Border

Naema, the Witch

In the Castle of Scotland (Trilogy 2)

New Era

Elixir of life

Pharaoh Mernephtah

The Legislators

The Magicians

The Terrible Ghost

Paradise without Adan

Romance of a Queen

Books of Arandi Gomes Texeira and JW Rochester

The Power of Love

Lancaster County

The Trial

Cleopatra's Bracelet

The Reincarnation of a Queen

You are Gods!

Books of Eliana Machado Coelho and Schellida

Aimless Hearts

The Brightness of Truth

The Right to Be Happy

The Return

In the Silence of Passions

Strength to Start Over

The Certainty of Victory

Conquest of Peace

Lessons that Life Provides

Stronger Than Ever

No Rules to Love

A Diary Through Time

A reason to Live

Eliana Machado Coelho and Schellida, Romances that captivate, teach, move and can change your life!

Books of Elisa Masselli

There is always a Reason

Nothing is Left without Answers

Life is Made by Decisions

The Mission of Each One

Something More is Needed

When the Past does not Matter

Destiny in your Hands

God is with him

When the Past does not Pass

Just Beginning

Books of Vera Lúcia Marinzeck de Carvalho and Patricia

Violets on the Window
Living in the Spirit World
The Writer's House
The Flight of the Seagull

Vera Lúcia Marinzeck de Carvalho and Antônio Carlos

Love your Enemies
Sale Bernardino
The Lovers' Rock
Rosa, the Third Fatality
Captives and Freed

Books of Mónica de Castro and Leonel

Despite Everything

Love is not to be trifled with

Face to Face with the Truth

Of my Whole Being

Desire

The Price of Being Different

Twins

Giselle, the Inquisitor's Mistress

Greta

Until Life Set Them Apart

Impulses of the Heart

Jurema of the Jungle

The Actress

The Power of Fate

Memories that the Wind Brings

Soul Secrets

Feeling in Your Skin

Zibia Gasparetto's Greatest Hits

With more than 20 million titles sold, the author has contributed to the strengthening of spiritualist literature in the editorial market and to the popularization of spirituality. Learn more of the author's hits.

Romances Dictated by the Spirit Lucius

The Force of Life

The Truth of Each Individual

Life Knows what it Does

She Trusted Life

Between Love and War

Esmeralda

Thorns of Time

Nothing is by Chance

Nobody Owns Nobody

God's Advocate

Tomorrow Belongs to God

Love Always Wins

Unexpected Encounter

The Thread of Destiny

The Matter

The Hill of Illusions

Where is Teresa?

A Doorway to the Heart

When Life Chooses
When the Time Comes
When it is Necessary to Return
Opening up for life
Not Afraid to Live
Only Love can do it
We are all Innocent
Everything Has its Price
Everything was Worthwhile
A Real Love
Overcoming the Past

World Spiritist Institute

www.ingramcontent.com/pod-product-compliance
Lightning Source LLC
LaVergne TN
LVHW041753060526
838201LV00046B/986